D0408063

For: **Joan**

My purpose is that [you] may be encouraged in heart and united in love, so that [you] may have the full riches of complete understanding, in order that [you] may know the mystery of God, namely, Christ.

COLOSSIANS 2:2

From: **Cynthia**

Thank you for your friendship. May you be blessed today and always.

with love

God's Words of Life on Marriage
© 2000 by Zondervan

ISBN 0-310-98358-4

Devotions excerpted from the NIV Marriage Devotional Bible.
Copyright 2000 by The Zondervan Corporation.

Requests for information should be addressed to:
    Inspirio, the Gift Group of Zondervan
    Grand Rapids, Michigan 49530

Associate Editor: Molly Detweiler
Project Editor: Pat Matuszak
Design Manager: Amy E. Langeler
Design: David Carlson

Printed in China

00 01 02 / HK / 4 3 2 1

GOD'S
WORDS OF
LIFE ON
Marriage

from the

NEW INTERNATIONAL
VERSION

inspirio

The gift group of Zondervan

GOD'S WORDS OF LIFE ON

Attitude

Be made new in the attitude of your minds ... put on the new self, created to be like God in true righteousness and holiness.

EPHESIANS 4:23–24

Your attitude should be the same as that of Christ Jesus: Who, being in very nature God, did not consider equality with God something to be grasped, but made himself nothing, taking the very nature of a servant, being made in human likeness.

PHILIPPIANS 2:5–7

Love is patient, love is kind. It does not envy, it does not boast, it is not proud. It is not rude, it is not self-seeking, it is not easily angered, it keeps no record of wrongs. Love does not delight in evil but rejoices with the truth. It always protects, always trusts, always hopes, always perseveres.

1 CORINTHIANS 13:4–7

Husbands, love your wives, just as Christ loved the church and gave himself up for her to make her holy, cleansing her by the washing with water through the word, and to present her to himself as a radiant church, without stain or wrinkle or any other blemish, but holy and blameless. In this same way, husbands ought to love their wives as their own bodies. He who loves his wife loves himself.

EPHESIANS 5:25–28

Be kind and compassionate to one another, forgiving each other, just as in Christ God forgave you. Be imitators of God, therefore, as dearly loved children and live a life of love, just as Christ loved us.

EPHESIANS 4:32—5:2

If you have any encouragement from being united with Christ, if any comfort from his love, if any fellowship with the Spirit, if any tenderness and compassion, then make my joy complete by being like-minded, having the same love, being one in spirit and purpose. Do nothing out of selfish ambition or vain conceit, but in humility consider others better than yourselves. Each of you should look not only to your own interests, but also to the interests of others.

PHILIPPIANS 2:1–4

Jesus said, "Love each other as I have loved you."

JOHN 15:12

Attitude

Be completely humble and gentle; be patient, bearing with one another in love. Make every effort to keep the unity of the Spirit through the bond of peace.

EPHESIANS 4:2–3

As God's chosen people, holy and dearly loved, clothe yourselves with compassion, kindness, humility, gentleness and patience. Bear with each other and forgive whatever grievances you may have against one another. Forgive as the Lord forgave you. And over all these virtues put on love, which binds them all together in perfect unity. Let the peace of Christ rule in your hearts, since as members of one body you were called to peace. And be thankful. Let the word of Christ dwell in you richly as you teach and admonish one another with all wisdom, and as you sing psalms, hymns and spiritual songs with gratitude in your hearts to God. And whatever you do, whether in word or deed, do it all in the name of the Lord Jesus, giving thanks to God the Father through him.

COLOSSIANS 3:12–17

Attitude

Each year as a couple, Bob and I have planned a "second" honeymoon trip. Sometimes it's a short trip to a bed and breakfast close to home, and sometimes it has been a spectacular event for which we prepare quite a while. Whether it is a small get-away or an eventful memory maker, it is always a time that helps us get back our perspective as a married couple. For a few days, we shed all our responsibilities and the roles we carry from work, or as parents, and just become lovers.

When we get bogged down in the daily grind or difficulties, let us never lose the perspective that we are headed to that marvelous destination. We are journeying through this life toward the New Jerusalem to share an eternity with Jesus Christ.

BOB AND ROSEMARY BARNES

If couples could be given a vaccine against pessimistic thinking, we would probably see the divorce rate all but drop off. In a sense, you can protect your marriage against this virus. All it takes is a good shot of optimism—rising above your circumstances and maintaining hope for your future.

LES AND LESLIE PARROTT

Change

God has said, "Never will I leave you; never will I forsake you."

So we say with confidence, "The LORD is my helper; I will not be afraid. What can man do to me?"...
Jesus Christ is the same yesterday and today and forever.

HEBREWS 13:5–8

We, who with unveiled faces all reflect the Lord's glory, are being transformed into his likeness with ever-increasing glory, which comes from the Lord, who is the Spirit.

2 CORINTHIANS 3:18

The plans of the LORD stand firm forever,
   the purposes of his heart through
   all generations.

PSALM 33:11

The LORD is a refuge for the oppressed,
   a stronghold in times of trouble.
Those who know your name will trust in you,
   for you, LORD, have never forsaken those
   who seek you.

PSALM 9:9–10

Change

We know that in all things God works for the good of those who love him, who have been called according to his purpose.

ROMANS 8:28

When I said, "My foot is slipping,"
　　your love, O LORD supported me.
When anxiety was great within me,
　　your consolation brought joy to my soul.

PSALM 94:18–19

The righteous stand firm forever. ...
The fear of the LORD adds length to life.. . .

PSALM 10:25, 27

Let all who take refuge in you be glad, O LORD;
　　let them ever sing for joy.
Spread your protection over them,
　　that those who love your name may rejoice in
　　you.
For surely, O LORD, you bless the righteous;
　　you surround them with your favor as with a
　　shield.

PSALM 5:11–12

Change

Our citizenship is in heaven. And we eagerly await a Savior from there, the Lord Jesus Christ, who, by the power that enables him to bring everything under his control, will transform our lowly bodies so that they will be like his glorious body.

PHILIPPIANS 3:20–21

Jesus said, "Do not let your hearts be troubled. Trust in God; trust also in me."

JOHN 14:1

Do not be anxious about anything, but in everything, by prayer and petition, with thanksgiving, present your requests to God. And the peace of God, which transcends all understanding, will guard your hearts and your minds in Christ Jesus.

PHILIPPIANS 4:6–7

Jesus Christ is the same yesterday and today and forever.

HEBREWS 13:8

Change

Few couples have had a more difficult beginning in their marriage than Mary and Joseph (see Matthew 1:18–25, Luke 2:1–20). First of all, she was pregnant; many may have wanted her to be stoned or at least call off the wedding. Second, Joseph's business was probably under-financed when the decree went out from Caesar Augustus that all people were to be enrolled for a new taxing. Just what a young couple needed! Can you imagine what it must have been like for a girl in her mid-teens, more than eight months pregnant, to ride on the back of a donkey? On top of all this, there was no room in the inn!

Their rough beginning continued with an announcement that all boy babies under two would be slain. There were dozens of places where this new marriage could have wavered and fallen apart. But these two good people loved God and were determined to make their love secure.

MARRIAGE DEVOTIONAL BIBLE

Children

When they see among them their children,
    the work of my hands, they will keep my
    name holy.

ISAIAH 29:23–23

I prayed for this child, and the LORD has granted me
what I asked of him.

1 SAMUEL 1:27

"Lift up your eyes and look around;
    all your sons gather and come to you.
As surely as I live," declares the LORD,
    "you will wear them all as ornaments;
you will put them on, like a bride."

ISAIAH 49:18

You, LORD, created my inmost being;
    you knit me together in my mother's womb.

PSALM 139:13

May the LORD make you increase,
    both you and your children.
May you be blessed by the LORD,
    the Maker of heaven and earth.

PSALM 115:14–15

GOD'S WORDS OF LIFE ON
Children

The LORD has done great things for us,
    and we are filled with joy.

PSALM 126:3

I was young and now I am old,
    yet I have never seen the righteous forsaken
    or their children begging bread.
They are always generous and lend freely;
    their children will be blessed.

PSALM 37:25–26

I have no greater joy than to hear that my children
are walking in the truth.

3 JOHN 4

May the LORD bless you from Zion
    all the days of your life;
may you see the prosperity of Jerusalem,
    and may you live to see your children's chil-
    dren.

PSALM 128:5–6

Jesus said, "Whoever welcomes this little child in my
name welcomes me."

LUKE 9:48

GOD'S WORDS OF LIFE ON
Children

We are God's workmanship, created in Christ Jesus to do good works, which God prepared in advance for us to do.

EPHESIANS 2:10

Now the LORD was gracious to Sarah as he had said, and the LORD did for Sarah what he had promised. Sarah became pregnant and bore a son to Abraham in his old age, at the very time God had promised him.

Abraham gave the name Isaac to the son Sarah bore him. ... Sarah said, "God has brought me laughter, and everyone who hears about this will laugh with me." And she added, "Who would have said to Abraham that Sarah would nurse children? Yet I have borne him a son in his old age."

GENESIS 21:1–7

Your wife will be like a fruitful vine
        within your house;
your sons will be like olive shoots
        around your table.
Thus is the man blessed
        who fears the LORD.

PSALM 128:3–4

GOD'S WORDS OF LIFE ON
Children

Like arrows in the hands of a warrior
   are sons born in one's youth.
Blessed is the man
   whose quiver is full of them.
PSALM 127:4–5

A woman giving birth to a child has pain because
her time has come; but when her baby is born she
forgets the anguish because of her joy that a child is
born into the world.
JOHN 16:21

The LORD tends his flock like a shepherd:
   He gathers the lambs in his arms
and carries them close to his heart;
   he gently leads those that have young.
ISAIAH 40:11

God will love you and bless you and increase your
numbers. He will bless the fruit of your womb, the
crops of your land.
DEUTERONOMY 7:13

Children

Jesus said, "Your Father in heaven is not willing that any of these little ones should be lost."

MATTHEW 18:14

Love the LORD your God with all your heart and with all your soul and with all your strength. These commandments that I give you today are to be upon your hearts. Impress them on your children. Talk about them when you sit at home and when you walk along the road, when you lie down and when you get up. Tie them as symbols on your hands and bind them on your foreheads. Write them on the doorframes of your houses and on your gates.

DEUTERONOMY 6:5–9

Children

Mary was a wise mother—she took time to "treasure all these things in her heart." In today's fast-paced world, time for reflection and treasuring the parenting process is rare. But if cultivated, this habit can enrich your role as partners.

As new parents, Dave and I remember gazing at our sleeping infant and suddenly realizing that this little one was a witness to our love for each other. As our three sons became toddlers, preschoolers and then entered the elementary years, they motivated us to be more creative in finding time for each other. They challenged our communication; when little ears were listening, we were more intentional in choosing our words. In the struggles of parenting adolescents, we found strength in our marriage relationship.

Now in the empty nest, our memories are precious. Many times it's the simple things we treasure the most. Taking a moment to enjoy a lovely sunset, the thrill of seeing the first daffodil, or recording some of the cute things a grandchild tells us over the phone all add to our treasure chest.

Appreciating the simple things in life will add to your own treasure chest of memories. Consider journaling some of the wonderful, ordinary and precious times you have together. Keep a log of your children's cute sayings and the funny things they do. Fill your own treasure chest.

Dave and Claudia Arp

Commitment

Trust in the LORD and do good;
  dwell in the land and enjoy safe pasture.
Delight yourself in the LORD
  and he will give you the desires of your heart.
Commit your way to the LORD;
  trust in him and he will do this:
He will make your righteousness shine like the
  dawn,
  the justice of your cause like the noonday sun.
Be still before the LORD and wait patiently for him.

PSALM 37:3–7

May the Lord direct your hearts into God's love and
Christ's perseverance.

2 THESSALONIANS 3:5

Love must be sincere. Hate what is evil; cling to
what is good. Be devoted to one another in brotherly love. Honor one another above yourselves.
Never be lacking in zeal, but keep your spiritual fervor, serving the Lord. Be joyful in hope, patient in
affliction, faithful in prayer.

ROMANS 12:9–12

GOD'S WORDS OF LIFE ON
Commitment

Commit to the LORD whatever you do,
    and your plans will succeed.

PROVERBS 16:3

Let us not become weary in doing good, for at the
proper time we will reap a harvest if we do not give up.

GALATIANS 6:9

Place me like a seal over your heart,
    like a seal on your arm; ...
Many waters cannot quench love;
    rivers cannot wash it away.

SONG OF SONGS 8:6–7

Then the LORD God made a woman from the rib he
had taken out of the man, and he brought her to the
man. The man said, "This is now bone of my bones
and flesh of my flesh; she shall be called 'woman,' for
she was taken out of man." For this reason a man
will leave his father and mother and be united to his
wife, and they will become one flesh.

GENESIS 2:22–24

The eyes of the LORD range throughout the earth to
strengthen those whose hearts are fully committed to
him.

2 CHRONICLES 16:9

Commitment

I commit you to God and to the word of his grace, which can build you up and give you an inheritance among all those who are sanctified.

ACTS 20:32

Until I come, devote yourself to the public reading of Scripture, to preaching and to teaching. . . . Be diligent in these matters; give yourself wholly to them, so that everyone may see your progress. Watch your life and doctrine closely. Persevere in them, because if you do, you will save both yourself and your hearers.

1 TIMOTHY 4:13, 15–16

If you devote your heart to the LORD
and stretch out your hands to him, . . .
then you will lift up your face without shame;
you will stand firm and without fear.
You will surely forget your trouble,
recalling it only as waters gone by.

JOB 11:13, 15–16

Commitment

Diane had been married for a decade, and it had become a hard journey because her husband, Bill, was building his career and was hardly ever home. Bill's long hours at the office and weekly travel caused her to feel alienated and lonely. To add to Diane's discouragement, her friends had been urging her to abandon her difficult marriage. The world around her was saying, "It's ridiculous to stay committed to something that doesn't make you happy." The whole concept of commitment was confusing to Diane. She wondered why she found it so difficult to commit. Then she considered Noah and his level of commitment.

Noah made a commitment to God to build an ark. Noah hadn't committed to build the ark only until the job became difficult … his commitment wasn't even to an ark. His commitment was to God. To the pagan world around him, building an ark seemed incredibly foolish. And spending a lifetime working on it seemed even more foolish.

Building a marriage in today's world can often seem as difficult as Noah's project. How does one stay with that commitment when the going gets tough?

Diane had to refocus her commitment to God, the One who created the plan, rather than to the project at hand. Instead of complaining, she focused her energy on making the times Bill was home as meaningful as she could. Daily she asked God to bring Bill's heart home. Her commitment to God kept her focused during this long, often lonely "building project."

BOB AND ROSEMARY BARNES

Communication

Let the peace of Christ rule in your hearts, since as members of one body you were called to peace. And be thankful.

COLOSSIANS 3:15

Love does no harm to its neighbor. Therefore love is the fulfillment of the law.

ROMANS 13:10

The good man brings good things out of the good stored up in his heart, ... For out of the overflow of his heart his mouth speaks.

LUKE 6:45

Let the word of Christ dwell in you richly as you teach and admonish one another with all wisdom, and as you sing psalms, hymns and spiritual songs with gratitude in your hearts to God.

COLOSSIANS 3:16

If I speak in the tongues of men and of angels, but have not love, I am only a resounding gong or a clanging cymbal.

1 CORINTHIANS 13:1

Communication

Do not let any unwholesome talk come out of your mouths, but only what is helpful for building others up according to their needs, that it may benefit those who listen.

EPHESIANS 4:29

My purpose is that they may be encouraged in heart and united in love, so that they may have the full riches of complete understanding, in order that they may know the mystery of God, namely, Christ, in whom are hidden all the treasures of wisdom and knowledge.

COLOSSIANS 2:2–3

Whoever would love life
    and see good days
must keep his tongue from evil
    and his lips from deceitful speech.
He must turn from evil and do good;
    he must seek peace and pursue it.
For the eyes of the Lord are on the righteous
    and his ears are attentive to their prayer.

1 PETER 3:10–12

Communication

Whatever you do, whether in word or deed, do it all in the name of the Lord Jesus, giving thanks to God the Father through him.

COLOSSIANS 3:17

I do not hide your righteousness in my heart,
O LORD;
I speak of your faithfulness and salvation.
I do not conceal your love and your truth. ...

PSALM 40:10

My mouth will speak words of wisdom;
the utterance from my heart will give
understanding.

PSALM 49:3

DEVOTIONAL THOUGHT ON

Communication

"It's not logical!" one says. The other responds, "What does logic have to do with it?" Both say, "If only you could understand me!"

Spouses misunderstand each other daily. In radio terms it's like one is talking on an AM channel and the other on an FM channel. Communication problems are nothing new—people at the tower of Babel had to deal with them, and so do spouses today.

Certainly the world would be a simpler place if everyone spoke the same language, and marriage would be easier if spouses always understood each other. But if you spoke the same "language" and always agreed with each other, your marriage could become very boring. Also, it could be tempting to take all the credit—instead of giving it to God. But not worry; we all know that marriage doesn't work that way.

As we seek to understand each other, we have the opportunity to trust God in a tangible way that honors him. Instead of being consumed with "building our own edifice," we need to seek to understand our spouse. In so doing, we can build a loving, transparent relationship that demonstrates to others the reality of God's grace and goodness.

DAVE AND CLAUDIA ARP

GOD'S WORDS OF LIFE ON
Contentment

You guide me with your counsel,
    and afterward you will take me into glory.
Whom have I in heaven but you?
    And earth has nothing I desire besides you.
My flesh and my heart may fail,
    but God is the strength of my heart
    and my portion forever.

PSALM 73:24–26

Jesus said, "Do not store up for yourselves treasures
on earth, where moth and rust destroy, and where
thieves break in and steal. But store up for yourselves
treasures in heaven. ... For where your treasure is,
there your heart will be also."

MATTHEW 6:19–21

I know what it is to be in need, and I know what it
is to have plenty. I have learned the secret of being
content in any and every situation, whether well fed
or hungry, whether living in plenty or in want. I can
do everything through Christ who gives me
strength.

PHILIPPIANS 4:12–13

GOD'S WORDS OF LIFE ON
Contentment

The LORD is my shepherd,
    I shall not be in want.
He makes me lie down in green pastures,
    he leads me beside quiet waters,
he restores my soul.
He guides me in paths of righteousness
    for his name's sake.

PSALM 23:1–3

My heart is not proud, O LORD,
    my eyes are not haughty;
I do not concern myself with great matters
    or things too wonderful for me.
But I have stilled and quieted my soul;
    like a weaned child with its mother,
    like a weaned child is my soul within me.
O Israel, put your hope in the LORD
    both now and forevermore.

PSALM 131

The righteous eat to their hearts' content.

PROVERBS 13:25

The fear of the LORD leads to life:
    Then one rests content, untouched by trouble.

PROVERBS 19:23

Contentment

Godliness with contentment is great gain.

1 TIMOTHY 6:6

Those who have served well gain an excellent standing and great assurance in their faith in Christ Jesus.

1 TIMOTHY 3:13

Jesus said, "Why do you worry about clothes? See how the lilies of the field grow. They do not labor or spin. Yet I tell you that not even Solomon in all his splendor was dressed like one of these. If that is how God clothes the grass of the field, which is here today and tomorrow is thrown into the fire, will he not much more clothe you? ... So do not worry, saying, 'What shall we eat?' or 'What shall we drink?' or 'What shall we wear?' For ... your heavenly Father knows that you need them. But seek first his kingdom and his righteousness, and all these things will be given to you as well."

MATTHEW 6:28–33

DEVOTIONAL THOUGHT ON
Contentment

PSALM 131

Purchasing a new house is exciting. The wait before moving in seems to take a lifetime. We think about finally having more space ... enough to last forever. When the day finally arrives, the effort of moving is worth it. After all, this is a dream come true, right?

Months later, when visiting a friend in his new house, we start to feel different. The friend's house has the extra garage or laundry room that you really wanted in your house. The house you loved when you first moved in is no longer quite as wonderful. What happened?

It might be a house, a car or any other once-desired possession. It might even be a marriage relationship once the first rush of emotion is over, we need to find contentment. Contentment is a choice that is made despite the temptation to be ruled by feelings. Feelings can change overnight, especially when we compare our lives with what other people have. Psalm 131:2 indicates that contentment is also an action. Having a still and quieted soul is what the psalmist has chosen.

Contentment is an ongoing choice to be happy with what we have and it will bring long-term happiness.

BOB AND ROSEMARY BARNES

GOD'S WORDS OF LIFE ON
Courage

My soul finds rest in God alone;
  my salvation comes from him.
He alone is my rock and my salvation;
  he is my fortress, I will never be shaken.
PSALM 62:1

Do not be anxious about anything, but in everything, by prayer and petition, with thanksgiving, present your requests to God. And the peace of God, which transcends all understanding, will guard your hearts and your minds in Christ Jesus.
PHILIPPIANS 4:6–7

Those who trust in the LORD are like Mount Zion,
  which cannot be shaken but endures forever.
PSALM 125:1

Jesus said, "I have told you these things, so that in me you may have peace. In this world you will have trouble. But take heart! I have overcome the world."
JOHN 16:33

When anxiety was great within me,
  your consolation brought joy to my soul,
  O LORD.
PSALM 94:19

Courage

Strengthen the feeble hands,
    steady the knees that give way;
say to those with fearful hearts,
    "Be strong, do not fear;
your God will come."

ISAIAH 35:3–4

Be strong and courageous. Do not be afraid or terrified because of them, for the LORD your God goes with you; he will never leave you nor forsake you.

DEUTERONOMY 31:6

I eagerly expect and hope that I will in no way be ashamed, but will have sufficient courage so that now as always Christ will be exalted in my body. ...

PHILIPPIANS 1:20

Christ is faithful as a son over God's house. And we are his house, if we hold on to our courage and the hope of which we boast.

HEBREWS 3:6

Because the hand of the LORD my God was on me, I took courage. ...

EZRA 7:28

Courage

Cast all your anxiety on God because he cares for you.

1 PETER 5:7

Jesus said, "Do not be afraid of what you are about to suffer. ... Be faithful, even to the point of death, and I will give you the crown of life."

REVELATION 2:10

There is no fear in love. But perfect love drives out fear. ...

1 JOHN 4:18

The Lord is my helper; I will not be afraid.
    What can man do to me?

HEBREWS 13:6

Whatever happens, conduct yourselves in a manner worthy of the gospel of Christ. Then ... I will know that you stand firm in one spirit, contending as one man for the faith of the gospel without being frightened in any way by those who oppose you. This is a sign to them that they will be destroyed, but that you will be saved—and that by God.

PHILIPPIANS 1:27–28

Courage

You did not receive a spirit that makes you a slave again to fear, but you received the Spirit of sonship. And by him we cry, "*Abba*, Father." The Spirit himself testifies with our spirit that we are God's children.

ROMANS 8:15–16

Jesus said, "Do not be afraid, little flock, for your Father has been pleased to give you the kingdom."

LUKE 12:32

One night the Lord spoke to Paul in a vision: "Do not be afraid; keep on speaking, do not be silent. For I am with you, and no one is going to attack and harm you, because I have many people in this city." So Paul stayed for a year and a half, teaching them the word of God.

ACTS 18:9–11

Jesus said, "Are not five sparrows sold for two pennies? Yet not one of them is forgotten by God. Indeed, the very hairs of your head are all numbered. Don't be afraid; you are worth more than many sparrows."

LUKE 12:6–7

Courage

The LORD, the King of Israel, is with you;
>   never again will you fear any harm.

ZEPHANIAH 3:15

I have set the LORD always before me.
>   Because he is at my right hand,
>   I will not be shaken.
Therefore my heart is glad and my tongue rejoices;
>   my body will also rest secure ...
You have made known to me the path of life;
>   you will fill me with joy in your presence,
>   with eternal pleasures at your right hand.

PSALM 16:8–9,11

Courage

Joshua faced a huge job in Deuteronomy 31:6. How would you like to be the one to fill Moses shoes? But God promised not only to be with Joshua but also to go before him, never leaving or forsaking him.

That same promise of God's abiding presence holds true today for you and your spouse. At times when your marriage must cross "the Jordan," when you feel overwhelmed, remember God is the one who strengthens you and gives you courage. He will never leave you or forsake you, and he will keep going before you and make a path for you to follow.

When stressful times come, you can choose to trust and not be afraid. In a culture where divorce runs rampant and some view "starter marriages" like "starter homes," you can surmount each challenge in your marriage with the confidence that the Lord not only is with you but is actually going before you.

DAVE AND CLAUDIA ARP

Decisions

"For I know the plans I have for you," declares the LORD, "plans to prosper you and not to harm you, plans to give you a hope and a future."

JEREMIAH 29:11

The LORD changes times and seasons. . . . He gives wisdom to the wise and knowledge to the discerning.

DANIEL 2:21

"I will instruct you and teach you in the way you
    should go;
    I will counsel you and watch over you," says
    the LORD.

PSALM 32:8

In your unfailing love you will lead
    the people you have redeemed, O LORD.
In your strength you will guide them
    to your holy dwelling.

EXODUS 15:13

Guide me in your truth and teach me,
    for you are God my Savior,
    and my hope is in you all day long.

PSALM 25:5

Decisions

By wisdom the LORD laid the earth's foundations,
    by understanding he set the heavens in place;
by his knowledge the deeps were divided,
    and the clouds let drop the dew. . . .
Preserve sound judgment and discernment,
    do not let them out of your sight;
they will be life for you,
    an ornament to grace your neck.
Then you will go on your way in safety,
    and your foot will not stumble;
when you lie down, you will not be afraid;
    when you lie down, your sleep will be sweet.
Have no fear of sudden disaster
    or of the ruin that overtakes the wicked,
for the LORD will be your confidence
    and will keep your foot from being snared.

PROVERBS 3:19–26

The LORD guides the humble in what is right
    and teaches them his way.
All the ways of the LORD are loving and faithful
    for those who keep the demands of his
    covenant.

PSALM 25:9–10

Decisions

Send forth your light and your truth, O LORD,
    let them guide me.

PSALM 43:3

The law of the LORD is perfect,
    reviving the soul.
The statutes of the LORD are trustworthy,
    making wise the simple.
The precepts of the LORD are right,
    giving joy to the heart.
The commands of the LORD are radiant,
    giving light to the eyes.

PSALM 19:7–8

Teach us to number our days aright,
    that we may gain a heart of wisdom.

PSALM 90:12

The fear of the LORD is the beginning of wisdom;
    all who follow his precepts have good under-
    standing.

PSALM 111:10

Direct my footsteps according to your word, O LORD.

PSALM 119:133

GOD'S WORDS OF LIFE ON
Decisions

All Scripture is God-breathed and is useful for teaching, rebuking, correcting and training in righteousness, so that the man of God may be thoroughly equipped for every good work.

2 TIMOTHY 3:16–17

If any of you lacks wisdom, he should ask God, who gives generously to all without finding fault, and it will be given to him.

JAMES 1:5

I am the LORD your God,
>   who teaches you what is best for you,
>   who directs you in the way you should go.

ISAIAH 48:17

Whether you turn to the right or to the left, your ears will hear a voice behind you, saying, "This is the way; walk in it."

ISAIAH 30:21

Teach me knowledge and good judgment, O LORD,
>   for I believe in your commands.

PSALM 119:66

Decisions

For the LORD gives wisdom,
and from his mouth come knowledge and
understanding.

PROVERBS 2:6

God, who said, "Let light shine out of darkness,"
made his light shine in our hearts to give us the light
of the knowledge of the glory of God in the face of
Christ.

2 CORINTHIANS 4:6

Hold on to instruction, do not let it go;
guard it well, for it is your life.

PROVERBS 4:13

Make plans by seeking advice.

PROVERBS 20:18

Decisions

JAMES 4:14

A number of years ago when we were making a shift in our ministry focus, we made two lists. The first was a list of things we had planned and the accompanying results. The second list was things we didn't plan, but that God dropped in our lap and the results. Guess which list was the most significant?

The God-initiated plans were the ones with the lasting impact. We now have what we affectionately call our "lap page" where we record God's plans. These are the things he brings into our life. Then we make "our plans" around his.

The Bible never discourages us from planning, preparing and looking expectantly toward the future. But James gives one important qualification: As we make our plans, whether in our personal lives, business or our marriage, we need to plan with the perspective that it is God who ultimately holds the future. James encourages us to say, "If it is the Lord's will, we will live and do this or that."

Actually, knowing God will have the final say is reassuring—especially when things don't go as we planned. Have you recently experienced a change of plans? In the middle of broken plans, we can experience his peace. We can know for certain that our infinitely wise and loving heavenly Father is in control of our lives and our circumstances.

DAVE AND CLAUDIA ARP

Differences

There are different kinds of gifts, but the same
Spirit. There are different kinds of service, but the
same Lord. There are different kinds of working, but
the same God works all of them in all men. Now to
each one the manifestation of the Spirit is given for
the common good.

1 CORINTHIANS 12:4–7

As God's chosen people, holy and dearly loved,
clothe yourselves with compassion, kindness,
humility, gentleness, and patience. Bear with each
other and forgive whatever grievances you may
have against one another. Forgive as the Lord forgave you.

COLOSSIANS 3:12–13

Two are better than one,
>   because they have a good return
>   for their work:
If one falls down,
>   his friend can help him up.

ECCLESIASTES 4:9–10

Jesus said, "Where two or three come together in my
name, there am I with them."

MATTHEW 18:20

Differences

He who covers over an offense promotes love,
  but whoever repeats the matter separates
  close friends.

PROVERBS 17:9

You are all sons of God through faith in Christ Jesus,
for all of you who were baptized into Christ have
clothed yourselves with Christ. There is neither Jew
nor Greek, slave nor free, male nor female, for you
are all one in Christ Jesus.

GALATIANS 3:26–28

To one there is given through the Spirit the message
of wisdom, to another the message of knowledge by
means of the same Spirit, to another faith by the
same Spirit, to another gifts of healing by that one
Spirit, to another miraculous powers, to another
prophecy, to another distinguishing between spirits,
to another speaking in different kinds of tongues,
and to still another the interpretation of tongues. All
these are the work of one and the same Spirit, and
he gives them to each one, just as he determines.

1 CORINTHIANS 12:8–11

Differences

Confess your sins to each other and pray for each other so that you may be healed.

JAMES 5:16

The body is a unit, though it is made up of many parts; and though all its parts are many, they form one body. So it is with Christ. For we were all baptized by one Spirit into one body—whether Jews or Greeks, slave or free—and we were all given the one Spirit to drink.

1 CORINTHIANS 12:12

God has arranged the parts in the body, every one of them, just as he wanted them to be. If they were all one part, where would the body be? As it is, there are many parts, but one body.

1 CORINTHIANS 12:18–20

DEVOTIONAL THOUGHT ON

Differences

The marriage of two different people means two different sets of ideas. No one can prepare us enough for the challenges we face in a marriage where two people are so different, even opposite in many areas. For example, Rosemary and I disagree dramatically about what makes a great Friday night. Having been out of the house all week, I prefer to stay at home. Rosemary, on the other hand, prefers to get out of the house she's been in all week and participate in a social activity.

Acknowledging differing opinions is the beginning of growth. And dealing with conflicting ideas and thoughts is the road toward growth together as a couple.

Believe it or not, conflicts in marriage can be helpful. But they are only helpful if handled the proper way. Talking about the conflict is a must. We need to talk about it together, rather than behind each other's backs.

Consider the way God handled the conflict in Numbers 12. Miriam and Aaron criticized Moses' choice of spouse. At once God brought Moses, Miriam and Aaron into the Tent of Meeting so he could spend time alone with them. The principle of confrontation is the key to observe here in this passage. Everyone involved was brought together to work out the problem.

BOB AND ROSEMARY BARNES

Difficult Times

God's compassions never fail.
They are new every morning;
   great is your faithfulness.
LAMENTATIONS 3:22–23

Jesus said, "I will show you what he is like who
comes to me and hears my words and puts them
into practice.
He is like a man building a house, who dug down
deep and laid the foundation on rock. When a flood
came, the torrent struck that house but could not
shake it, because it was well built.
But the one who hears my words and does not put
them into practice is like a man who built a house
on the ground without a foundation. The moment
the torrent struck that house, it collapsed and its
destruction was complete."
LUKE 6:47–49

For God has not despised or disdained
   the suffering of the afflicted one;
he has not hidden his face from him
   but has listened to his cry for help.
PSALM 22:24

Difficult Times

In my distress I called to the LORD;
>   I cried to my God for help.
From his temple he heard my voice;
>   my cry came before him, into his ears. . . .
He parted the heavens and came down;
>   dark clouds were under his feet.
He mounted the cherubim and flew;
>   he soared on the wings of the wind. . . .
The LORD thundered from heaven;
>   the voice of the Most High resounded.
He shot his arrows and scattered the enemies,
>   great bolts of lightning and routed them. . . .
He reached down from on high and took hold of me;
>   he drew me out of deep waters.
He rescued me from my powerful enemy,
>   from my foes, who were too strong for me. . . .
He brought me out into a spacious place;
>   he rescued me because he delighted in me.

PSALM 18:6, 9–10, 13–14, 16–17, 19

O LORD my God, I called to you for help
>   and you healed me.

PSALM 30:2

Difficult Times

In my alarm I said,
> "I am cut off from your sight!"
Yet you heard my cry for mercy
> when I called to you for help.
Love the LORD, all his saints!
> The LORD preserves the faithful. ...
Be strong and take heart,
> all you who hope in the LORD.

PSALM 31:22–24

You are my hiding place, O LORD;
> you will protect me from trouble
> and surround me with songs of deliverance.

PSALM 32:7

Let all who take refuge in you be glad;
> let them ever sing for joy.
Spread your protection over them,
> that those who love your name may rejoice in
> you.
For surely, O LORD, you bless the righteous;
> you surround them with your favor as with a
> shield.

PSALM 5:11–12

GOD'S WORDS OF LIFE ON
Difficult Times

God is our refuge and strength,
an ever-present help in trouble.

PSALM 46:1

Let us ... approach the throne of grace with confidence, so that we may receive mercy and find grace to help us in our time of need.

HEBREWS 4:16

"Because he loves me," says the LORD, "I will rescue him;
I will protect him, for he acknowledges my name.
He will call upon me, and I will answer him;
I will be with him in trouble,
I will deliver him and honor him.
With long life will I satisfy him
and show him my salvation."

PSALM 91:14–16

The Lord is faithful, and he will strengthen and protect you from the evil one.

2 THESSALONIANS 3:3

GOD'S WORDS OF LIFE ON
Difficult Times

The God of all grace, who called you to his eternal
glory in Christ, after you have suffered a little while,
will himself restore you and make you strong, firm
and steadfast. To him be the power for ever and ever.
1 PETER 5:10–11

The LORD is my shepherd, I shall not be in want.
He makes me lie down in green pastures,
   he leads me beside quiet waters,
   he restores my soul.
He guides me in paths of righteousness
   for his name's sake.
Even though I walk
   through the valley of the shadow of death,
I will fear no evil,
   for you are with me;
your rod and your staff,
   they comfort me.
You prepare a table before me
   in the presence of my enemies.
You anoint my head with oil;
   my cup overflows.
Surely goodness and love will follow me
   all the days of my life,
and I will dwell in the house of the LORD
   forever.
PSALM 23

Difficult Times

When our first baby arrived, she turned our home into a foreign land. We were exhausted and didn't have any time alone together. Intimacy seemed non-existent. This was a time that we learned to study God's word in a more intense way than ever before, believing that he would be our source of happiness.

When life [is difficult], God will use it for good to accomplish what he wants in your life and that "in all things God works for the good of those who love him" (Romans 8:28). When you are in circumstances that seem to place you in that "foreign land," remember to place your trust in God alone.

BOB AND ROSEMARY BARNES

All of us from time to time face news that is less than thrilling, but in Psalm 112:4–7 we read that "Even in the darkness light dawns for the upright." ... The one who is trusting in the Lord knows, even during tragedy, God will see him or her through.

DAVE AND CLAUDIA ARP

GOD'S WORDS OF LIFE ON
Encouragement

Let us not give up meeting together, as some are in the habit of doing, but let us encourage one another.

HEBREWS 10:25

Your love has given me great joy and encouragement.

PHILEMON 1:7

May our Lord Jesus Christ himself and God our Father, who loved us and by his grace gave us eternal encouragement and good hope, encourage your hearts and strengthen you in every good deed and word.

2 THESSALONIANS 2:16–17

The LORD himself goes before you and will be with you; he will never leave you nor forsake you. Do not be afraid; do not be discouraged.

DEUTERONOMY 31:8

You are a shield around me, O LORD;
    you bestow glory on me and lift up my head.

PSALM 3:3

GOD'S WORDS OF LIFE ON
Encouragement

Encourage one another and build each other up, just as in fact you are doing.

1 THESSALONIANS 5:11

My purpose is that they may be encouraged in heart and united in love, so that they may have the full riches of complete understanding, in order that they may know the mystery of God, namely, Christ, in whom are hidden all the treasures of wisdom and knowledge.

COLOSSIANS 2:2–3

I lift up my eyes to the hills—
    where does my help come from?
My help comes from the LORD,
    the Maker of heaven and earth.
He will not let your foot slip—
    he who watches over you will not slumber;
indeed, he who watches over Israel
    will neither slumber nor sleep.

PSALM 121:1–4

Encourage one another daily.

HEBREWS 3:13

Encouragement

Let the morning bring me word
    of your unfailing love, O LORD,
    for I have put my trust in you.
Show me the way I should go,
    for to you I lift up my soul.

PSALM 143:8

May the God who gives endurance and encouragement give you a spirit of unity among yourselves as
you follow Christ Jesus, so that with one heart and
mouth you may glorify the God and Father of our
Lord Jesus Christ.

ROMANS 15:5–6

It is God who arms me with strength
    and makes my way perfect.
He makes my feet like the feet of a deer;
    he enables me to stand on the heights.

PSALM 18:32–33

Why are you downcast, O my soul?
    Why so disturbed within me?
Put your hope in God,
    for I will yet praise him,
    my Savior and my God.

PSALM 42:5–6

Encouragement

On a recent trip to the New England coast, we discovered a little lighthouse that has been a source of encouragement for many lonely sailors over the years. Monot's light, near Scituate, Massachusetts, signals the nautical code that spells "I love you." Wives in this sailing town sent out this message to encourage their husbands out at sea and remind them how much they were loved.

Several years ago the Coast Guard decided to upgrade the light ... and for technical reasons the new machines would be unable to flash the "I love you" message. Both the families waiting in town and the sailors protested. The Coast Guard finally weakened. The old equipment ... was reinstalled.

Every spouse needs an encouraging word. More than that, we need a marriage that serves as a kind of safe harbor, a place where we can count on being encouraged. Encourage each other today!

LES AND LESLIE PARROTT

Faithfulness

The LORD, the LORD, the compassionate and gracious God, slow to anger, abounding in love and faithfulness, maintaining love to thousands, and forgiving ... sin.

EXODUS 34:6–7

The LORD rewards every man for his righteousness and faithfulness.

1 SAMUEL 26:23

To the faithful you show yourself faithful, O LORD,
    to the blameless you show yourself blameless.

2 SAMUEL 22:26

God, who has called you into fellowship with his Son Jesus Christ our Lord, is faithful.

1 CORINTHIANS 1:9

The LORD preserves the faithful.

PSALM 31:23

Your love, O LORD, reaches to the heavens,
    your faithfulness to the skies.

PSALM 36:5

Faithfulness

The LORD loves the just
> and will not forsake his faithful ones.

PSALM 37:28

Love and faithfulness meet together;
> righteousness and peace kiss each other.
Faithfulness springs forth from the earth,
> and righteousness looks down from heaven.

PSALM 85:10–11

I will sing of the LORD's great love forever;
> with my mouth I will make your faithfulness
> known through all generations.
I will declare that your love stands firm forever,
> that you established your faithfulness in
> heaven itself.

PSALM 89:1–2

Because of the LORD's great love we are not
> consumed,
> for his compassions never fail.
They are new every morning;
> great is your faithfulness.

LAMENTATIONS 3:22–23

GOD'S WORDS OF LIFE ON
Faithfulness

Let love and faithfulness never leave you;
    bind them around your neck,
    write them on the tablet of your heart.
Then you will win favor and a good name
    in the sight of God and man.

PROVERBS 3:3–4

Through love and faithfulness sin is atoned for;
    through the fear of the LORD a man avoids
    evil.

PROVERBS 16:6

A faithful man will be richly blessed.

PROVERBS 28:20

If we confess our sins, God is faithful and just and
will forgive us our sins and purify us from all
unrighteousness.

1 JOHN 1:9

Each one should use whatever gift he has received to
serve others, faithfully administering God's grace in
its various forms.

1 PETER 4:10

Faithfulness

Let us hold unswervingly to the hope we profess, for God who promised is faithful.

HEBREWS 10:23

The Lord is faithful, and he will strengthen and protect you from the evil one.

2 THESSALONIANS 3:3

May God himself, the God of peace, sanctify you through and through. May your whole spirit, soul and body be kept blameless at the coming of our Lord Jesus Christ. The one who calls you is faithful and he will do it.

1 THESSALONIANS 5:23–24

The fruit of the Spirit is love, joy, peace, patience, kindness, goodness, faithfulness, gentleness and self-control.

GALATIANS 5:22–23

God is faithful; he will not let you be tempted beyond what you can bear. But when you are tempted, he will also provide a way out so that you can stand up under it.

1 CORINTHIANS 10:13

Faithfulness

All the ways of the LORD are loving and faithful
    for those who keep the demands of his
    covenant.
PSALM 25:10

The LORD is faithful to all his promises
    and loving toward all he has made.
PSALM 145:13

O LORD, you are my God;
    I will exalt you and praise your name,
for in perfect faithfulness
    you have done marvelous things,
    things planned long ago.
ISAIAH 25:1

Faithfulness

Knowing that the Lord is trustworthy and faithful takes the edge off of life even when we let each other down—like the time Claudia got her hair cut too short. Rather than console her, I responded, "Makes you look older, doesn't it?" Or the time I procrastinated and missed an important IRS deadline and Claudia responded, "How could you be so careless? You let us both down this time."

God's faithfulness is a great backdrop for dealing with marital irritations. And even when you walk through more difficult situations ... he will give you the courage to work through them. ...

Life rushes by us. For us, in each passing decade, time seems to accelerate. The less of life there is to waste, the more precious it becomes and the more we need to rely upon God and his faithfulness to help our marriage grow.

DAVE AND CLAUDIA ARP

Finances

He who pursues righteousness and love
  finds life, prosperity and honor.

PROVERBS 21:21

God's divine power has given us everything we need
for life and godliness through our knowledge of him
who called us by his own glory and goodness.

2 PETER 1:3

God raises the poor from the dust
  and lifts the needy from the ash heap;
he seats them with princes
  and has them inherit a throne of honor.

1 SAMUEL 2:8

Humility and the fear of the LORD
  bring wealth and honor and life.

PROVERBS 22:4

Godliness with contentment is great gain. For we
brought nothing into the world, and we can take
nothing out of it.

1 TIMOTHY 6:6–7

Finances

Dishonest money dwindles away,
>   but he who gathers money little by little
>   makes it grow.

PROVERBS 13:11

Wisdom is a shelter
>   as money is a shelter,
but the advantage of knowledge is this:
>   that wisdom preserves the life of its possessor.

ECCLESIASTES 7:12

"Come, all you who are thirsty,
>   come to the waters;
and you who have no money,
>   come, buy and eat!
Come, buy wine and milk
>   without money and without cost.
Why spend money on what is not bread,
>   and your labor on what does not satisfy?
Listen, listen to me, and eat what is good,
>   and your soul will delight in the richest of
>   fare,"
>   says the LORD.

ISAIAH 55:1–2

GOD'S WORDS OF LIFE ON
Finances

Jesus sat down opposite the place where the offerings were put and watched the crowd putting their money into the temple treasury. Many rich people threw in large amounts. But a poor widow came and put in two very small copper coins, worth only a fraction of a penny.

Calling his disciples to him, Jesus said, "I tell you the truth, this poor widow has put more into the treasury than all the others. They all gave out of their wealth; but she, out of her poverty, put in everything—all she had to live on."

MARK 12:41–44

"Bring the whole tithe into the storehouse, that there may be food in my house. Test me in this," says the LORD Almighty, "and see if I will not throw open the floodgates of heaven and pour out so much blessing that you will not have room enough for it."

MALACHI 3:10

Finances

Martin Luther observed that there are three conversions necessary: the conversion of the heart, the mind and the purse. Of the three, the purse can be the most difficult. Agreeing on money matters can be tough, and, for many couples, agreeing on tithes and offerings presents a special challenge.

A fundamental shift in attitude toward giving took place in our home when we changed the question we were asking each other. Rather than, "How much of our money should we give to God," we learned to ask, "How much of God's money should we spend on ourselves?" The difference between these two questions was monumental for us. It helped us to remember that our financial resources are not partly ours and partly God's. Our income is all God's (see Exodus 19:5–6; Job 41:11; Psalm 24:1).

Although having this attitude is sometimes hard, especially when the bills pile up and the car needs to go to the mechanic—again! But if we trust in God, he will surely provide what we need to pay the bills ... and then again some.

LES AND LESLIE PARROTT

GOD'S WORDS OF LIFE ON
Forgiveness

If you, O LORD, kept a record of sins,
    O Lord, who could stand?
But with you there is forgiveness.
PSALM 130:3-4

Ask and it will be given to you; seek and you will
find; knock and the door will be opened to you. For
everyone who asks receives; he who seeks finds; and
to him who knocks, the door will be opened.
MATTHEW 7:7-8

Blessed are the merciful,
    for they will be shown mercy.
MATTHEW 5:7

Confess your sins to each other and pray for each
other so that you may be healed.
JAMES 5:16

Be imitators of God, ... as dearly loved children and
live a life full of love, just as Christ loved us and gave
himself up for us as a fragrant offering and sacrifice
to God.
EPHESIANS 5:1

GOD'S WORDS OF LIFE ON
Forgiveness

A man's wisdom gives him patience;
  it is to his glory to overlook an offense.
PROVERBS 19:11

When you stand praying, if you hold anything
against anyone, forgive him, so that your Father in
heaven may forgive you your sins.
MARK 11:25

Be kind and compassionate to one another, forgiving
each other, just as in Christ God forgave you.
EPHESIANS 4:32

Then Peter came to Jesus and asked, "Lord, how
many times shall I forgive my brother when he sins
against me? Up to seven times?"
Jesus answered, "I tell you, not seven times, but sev-
enty-seven times."
MATTHEW 18:21–22

If we confess our sins, God is faithful and just and
will forgive us our sins and purify us from all
unrighteousness.
1 JOHN 1:9

GOD'S WORDS OF LIFE ON
Forgiveness

Bear with each other and forgive whatever grievances you may have against one another. Forgive as the Lord forgave you. And over all these virtues put on love, which binds them all together in perfect unity. Let the peace of Christ rule in your hearts, since as members of one body you were called to peace. And be thankful.

COLOSSIANS 3:13–15

In Christ we have redemption through his blood, the forgiveness of sins, in accordance with the riches of God's grace that he lavished on us with all wisdom and understanding. And he made known to us the mystery of his will according to his good pleasure, which he purposed in Christ.

EPHESIANS 1:7–9

If anyone has caused grief ... you ought to forgive and comfort him, so that he will not be overwhelmed by excessive sorrow. I urge you, therefore, to reaffirm your love for him.

2 CORINTHIANS 2:5, 7–8

Forgiveness

Blessed are they whose transgressions are forgiven,
whose sins are covered. Blessed is the man whose sin
the Lord will never count against him.

ROMANS 4:7–8

Who is a God like you,
    who pardons sin and forgives the transgression
    of the remnant of his inheritance?
You do not stay angry forever
    but delight to show mercy.
You will again have compassion on us;
    you will tread our sins underfoot
    and hurl all our iniquities into the depths of
    the sea.

MICAH 7:18–19

Praise the LORD, O my soul,
    and forget not all his benefits—
who forgives all your sins
    and heals all your diseases,
who redeems your life from the pit
    and crowns you with love and compassion,
who satisfies your desires with good things
    so that your youth is renewed like the eagle's.

PSALM 103:2–5

Forgiveness

You are forgiving and good, O Lord,
    abounding in love to all who call to you.

PSALM 86:5

When we were overwhelmed by sins,
    you forgave our transgressions, O LORD.

PSALM 65:3

I acknowledged my sin to you
    and did not cover up my iniquity.
I said, "I will confess
    my transgressions to the LORD"—
and you forgave
    the guilt of my sin.

PSALM 32:5

Forgiveness

GENESIS 42–45

"Love means never having to say you're sorry" was a line in the popular 1960's movie *Love Story.* The wisdom of that phrase is debatable. But what's not debatable is that love means always having to forgive, even when your spouse fails to say "sorry."

The marriage relationship requires major doses of forgiveness. Whether it's forgiving differences in temperament or violations of trust, forgiveness is the bridge to getting over all those valleys.

You may ask, But what if my spouse hasn't asked for forgiveness yet? Can I forgive him before asks? That's where we learn a great lesson from Joseph.

When Joseph's brothers came to Egypt—the same brothers who had sold him into slavery—Joseph had a chance to seek vengeance. But obviously Joseph had already decided to forgive them, even though they hadn't yet asked. As a basic principle of relationships, God requires that we forgive those who have wronged us, whether they ask or not.

Each of us has the freedom and responsibility to choose to forgive those who have offended us. The intimacy of marriage includes many moments of hurt. Love does mean having to say we are sorry, but more importantly, love means choosing to forgive, even before we are asked.

BOB AND ROSEMARY BARNES

Friendship

This is my lover, this my friend.

SONG OF SONGS 5:16

A friend loves at all times.

PROVERBS 17:17

Perfume and incense bring joy to the heart,
and the pleasantness of one's friend springs from his
earnest counsel.

PROVERBS 27:9

Two are better than one,
because they have a good return for their work:
If one falls down,
his friend can help him up.
But pity the man who falls
and has no one to help him up!
Also, if two lie down together, they will keep warm.
But how can one keep warm alone?
Though one may be overpowered,
two can defend themselves.
A cord of three strands is not quickly broken.

ECCLESIASTES 4:9–12

Friendship

Carry each other's burdens, and in this way you will fulfill the law of Christ.

GALATIANS 6:2

Be devoted to one another in brotherly love. Honor one another above yourselves. Never be lacking in zeal, but keep your spiritual fervor, serving the Lord. Be joyful in hope, patient in affliction, faithful in prayer.

ROMANS 12:10–12

Dear friends, let us love one another, for love comes from God.

1 JOHN 4:7

Wounds from a friend can be trusted.

PROVERBS 27:6

A man of many companions may come to ruin,
      but there is a friend
who sticks closer than a brother.

PROVERBS 18:24

He who covers over an offense promotes love,
      but whoever repeats the matter
separates close friends.

PROVERBS 17:9

Friendship

Like a lily among thorns
    is my darling among the maidens.
Like an apple tree among the trees of the forest
    is my lover among the young men.
I delight to sit in his shade.

SONG OF SONGS 2:2–3

You have stolen my heart, my sister, my bride;
    you have stolen my heart
with one glance of your eyes,
    with one jewel of your necklace.
How delightful is your love, my sister, my bride!
    How much more pleasing is your love than
    wine,
    and the fragrance of your perfume than any
    spice!

SONG OF SONGS 4:9–10

Friendship

ECCLESIASTES 4:9–12

A Christian marriage is like a cord of three strands—the husband, the wife and God. Our faith in Jesus Christ gives us a common focus and helps to keep our marriage cord strong.

Years ago we chose Ecclesiastes 4:9–12 as our marriage passage. When viewed through a marriage filter, these verses give a wonderful picture of a Christian marriage. It's not a perfect relationship. The husband and wife fall down from time to time, but they willingly help each other up again. And even more important is the third strand. When both of our strands are frayed, God keeps our marriage cord strong. …

Like us, from time to time you will probably fall and let each other down, but God will remain faithful when you have a cord of three strands. When life gets hard, we can cope much better when we have a spouse-friend who will help with the challenges of life.

DAVE AND CLAUDIA ARP

Future Goals

"I know the plans I have for you," declares the LORD, "plans to prosper you and not to harm you, plans to give you hope and a future. Then you will call upon me and come and pray to me, and I will listen to you. You will seek me and find me when you seek me with all your heart."

JEREMIAH 29:11–13

Know also that wisdom is sweet to your soul;
    if you find it, there is a future hope for you,
    and your hope will not be cut off.

PROVERBS 24:14

In Christ we were also chosen, having been predestined according to the plan of him who works out everything in conformity with the purpose of his will, in order that we, who were the first to hope in Christ, might be for the praise of his glory.

EPHESIANS 1:11–12

Those who plan what is good find love and faithfulness.

PROVERBS 14:22

Future Goals

Many, O LORD my God,
>are the wonders you have done.

The things you planned for us
>no one can recount to you;

were I to speak and tell of them,
>they would be too many to declare.

PSALM 40:5

Delight yourself in the LORD
>and he will give you the desires of your heart.

PSALM 37:4

The LORD will fulfill his purpose for me;
>your love, O LORD, endures forever—
>do not abandon the works of your hands.

PSALM 138:8

As it is written:
"No eye has seen,
>no ear has heard,

no mind has conceived
>what God has prepared for those who love
>him"—

but God has revealed it to us by his Spirit. The Spirit searches all things, even the deep things of God.

1 CORINTHIANS 2:9–10

Future Goals

Store up for yourselves treasures in heaven, where moth and rust do not destroy, and where thieves do not break in and steal. For where your treasure is, there your heart will be also.

MATTHEW 6:20–21

Stand firm. Let nothing move you. Always give yourselves fully to the work of the Lord, because you know that your labor in the Lord is not in vain.

1 CORINTHIANS 15:58

The plans of the diligent lead to profit.

PROVERBS 21:5

Commit to the LORD whatever you do,
　　and your plans will succeed.

PROVERBS 16:3

Future Goals

The musical play *Man of La Mancha* is one of our all-time favorites. It is the story of a crazy old man ... one hundred years after the age of chivalry, when there are no more knights. But, thinking he is one, Don Quixote puts on a strange suit of armor and rides into the world to battle evil and protect the weak. ...

He calls the innkeeper the lord of a great castle. ... He pronounces a wretched [orphan] girl the great lady Dulcinea and begs for her handkerchief as a token to carry with him into battle.

Everyone thinks Don Quixote is bonkers, but at the end of the play the old man who is about to die is no longer suffering from these delusions. In a moving scene, all the people he has renamed appear at his bedside and beg him not to change. His excitement about their future has transformed them, and they have become the people that this insane visionary saw them to be.

The message of the play is simple: The dreams and hopes of the people around us powerfully shape our lives. And the message to married couples is that when you dream for each other will powerfully shape your marriage. What we consciously dream about, what we envision for our future together, the goals we set for our partnership, determine the quality of our marriage in the present. ... if our dreams are worthy and filled with godly hope, they can take us to heights we could never have imagined.

LES AND LESLIE PARROTT

Grace

Let your conversation be always full of grace, seasoned with salt, so that you may know how to answer everyone.

COLOSSIANS 4:6

Let the peace of Christ rule in your hearts, since as members of one body you were called to peace. And be thankful. Let the word of Christ dwell in you richly as you teach and admonish one another with all wisdom, and as you sing psalms, hymns and spiritual songs with gratitude in your hearts to God. And whatever you do, whether in word or deed, do it all in the name of the Lord Jesus, giving thanks to God the Father through him.

COLOSSIANS 3:15–17

Jesus said, "Love each other as I have loved you. Greater love has no one than this, that he lay down his life for his friends."

JOHN 15:12–13

From the fullness of God's grace we have all received one blessing after another.

JOHN 1:16

Grace

This righteousness from God comes through faith in Jesus Christ to all who believe. There is no difference, for all have sinned and fall short of the glory of God, and are justified freely by his grace through the redemption that came by Christ Jesus.

ROMANS 3:22–24

You know the grace of our Lord Jesus Christ, that though he was rich, yet for your sakes he became poor, so that you through his poverty might become rich.

2 CORINTHIANS 8:9

Since we have been justified through faith, we have peace with God through our Lord Jesus Christ, through whom we have gained access by faith into this grace in which we now stand. And we rejoice in the hope of the glory of God.

ROMANS 5:1–2

God is able to make all grace abound to you, so that in all things at all times, having all that you need, you will abound in every good work.

2 CORINTHIANS 9:8

Grace

God raised us up with Christ and seated us with him in the heavenly realms in Christ Jesus, in order that in the coming ages he might show the incomparable riches of his grace, expressed in his kindness to us in Christ Jesus.

EPHESIANS 2:6–7

If the many died by the trespass of the one man, how much more did God's grace and the gift that came by the grace of the one man, Jesus Christ, overflow to the many! ... For if, by the trespass of the one man, death reigned through that one man, how much more will those who receive God's abundant provision of grace and of the gift of righteousness reign in life through the one man, Jesus Christ.

ROMANS 5:15, 17

The Lord said to me, "My grace is sufficient for you, for my power is made perfect in weakness." Therefore I will boast all the more gladly about my weaknesses, so that Christ's power may rest on me. That is why, for Christ's sake, I delight in weaknesses, in insults, in hardships, in persecutions, in difficulties. For when I am weak, then I am strong.

2 CORINTHIANS 12:9–10

It is by grace you have been saved, through faith—and this not from yourselves, it is the gift of God—not by works, so that no one can boast. For we are God's workmanship, created in Christ Jesus to do good works, which God prepared in advance for us to do.

EPHESIANS 2:8–10

To each one of us grace has been given as Christ apportioned it.

EPHESIANS 4:7

When the kindness and love of God our Savior appeared, he saved us, not because of righteous things we had done, but because of his mercy. He saved us through the washing of rebirth and renewal by the Holy Spirit, whom he poured out on us generously through Jesus Christ our Savior, so that, having been justified by his grace, we might become heirs having the hope of eternal life.

TITUS 3:4–7

Let us ... approach the throne of grace with confidence, so that we may receive mercy and find grace to help us in our time of need.

HEBREWS 4:16

Grace

Praise be to the God and Father of our Lord Jesus Christ, who has blessed us in the heavenly realms with every spiritual blessing in Christ. For he chose us in him before the creation of the world to be holy and blameless in his sight. In love he predestined us to be adopted as his sons through Jesus Christ, in accordance with his pleasure and will—to the praise of his glorious grace, which he has freely given us in the One he loves. In him we have redemption through his blood, the forgiveness of sins, in accordance with the riches of God's grace that he lavished on us with all wisdom and understanding.

EPHESIANS 1:3–8

Grace

Although God gave the Ten Commandments to his people more than 3,000 years ago, they are still relevant today. Almost 1,500 years after God gave the laws, Jesus upheld them, calling them the "commandments" and listing five of them for the rich young ruler (see Matthew 19:16–19). And in the Sermon on the Mount, Jesus showed that his coming had not canceled the commandments.

Jesus actually placed these laws on a higher level by demanding that the spirit as well as the legal aspects of the law be kept (see Matthew 5:17–28).

That's an important message for married couples. How many times have you tagged your spouse off base for not following the rules—any rules? But consider this fact: God never intended for the Ten Commandments to be a set of regulations by which anyone would earn salvation. At the heart of the covenant relationship lay an act of divine grace.

This is a great reminder for couples. We need to offer the same kind of grace to one another—before we make accusations, point our fingers and demand justice. Laws always need to be balanced with love.

LES AND LESLIE PARROTT

Healing

Christ himself bore our sins in his body on the tree, so that we might die to sins and live for righteousness; by his wounds you have been healed.

1 PETER 2:24

Confess your sins to each other and pray for each other so that you may be healed. The prayer of a righteous man is powerful and effective.

JAMES 5:16

"For you who revere my name, the sun of righteousness will rise with healing in its wings," says the LORD.

MALACHI 4:2

Heal me, O LORD, and I will be healed;
    save me and I will be saved,
    for you are the one I praise.

JEREMIAH 17:14

Your light will break forth like the dawn,
    and your healing will quickly appear;
then your righteousness will go before you,
    and the glory of the LORD will be your rear
    guard.

ISAIAH 58:8

Healing

The Messiah was pierced for our transgressions,
>   he was crushed for our iniquities;
the punishment that brought us peace was upon
>   him,
>   and by his wounds we are healed.

ISAIAH 53:5

Pleasant words are a honeycomb,
>   sweet to the soul and healing to the bones.

PROVERBS 16:24

The LORD heals the brokenhearted
>   and binds up their wounds.

PSALM 147:3

Praise the LORD, O my soul,
>   and forget not all his benefits—
who forgives all your sins
>   and heals all your diseases,
who redeems your life from the pit
>   and crowns you with love and compassion,
who satisfies your desires with good things
>   so that your youth is renewed like the eagle's.

PSALM 103:2–5

GOD'S WORDS OF LIFE ON
Healing

The tongue that brings healing is a tree of life.

PROVERBS 15:4

O LORD my God, I called to you for help
    and you healed me.

PSALM 30:2

"If my people, who are called by my name, will
humble themselves and pray and seek my face and
turn from their wicked ways, then will I hear from
heaven and will forgive their sin and will heal their
land," says the LORD.

2 CHRONICLES 7:14

DEVOTIONAL THOUGHT ON
Healing

2 KINGS 5:1–14

Naaman was the commander of the army of the king of Aram. He was highly regarded and a valiant soldier, but he had leprosy. Fortunately his wife stood by him in sickness and took the initiative in seeking help. When her Israelite servant suggested that Naaman go see the prophet Elisha, she relayed the suggestion to her husband. Their relationship must have been one of open communication and trust, because he took her advice.

Maintaining a healthy marriage then and now is hard work—especially in the middle of health problems. … Think about how hard it must have been for Naaman and his wife to deal with his illness. He was a public figure, and everyone would have been aware of his leprosy. … Naaman's story had a happy ending. He went to Elisha, was healed of leprosy and found a new faith in God.

God can bring blessings out of difficult situations. If you are facing health problems or another difficult situation, follow the example of Naaman's wife. Be future focused, be positive and talk about it. You can trust God to meet your needs as you support each other.

MARRIAGE DEVOTIONAL BIBLE

91

GOD'S WORDS OF LIFE ON
Hope

I thank my God every time I remember you. ... I
always pray with joy because of your partnership in
the gospel from the first day until now, being confi-
dent of this, that he who began a good work in you
will carry it on to completion until the day of Christ
Jesus.

PHILIPPIANS 1:3–6

Let us draw near to God with a sincere heart in full
assurance of faith, having our hearts sprinkled to
cleanse us from a guilty conscience and having our
bodies washed with pure water. Let us hold
unswervingly to the hope we profess, for he who
promised is faithful. And let us consider how we
may spur one another on toward love and good
deeds. Let us not give up meeting together, as some
are in the habit of doing, but let us encourage one
another—and all the more as you see the Day
approaching.

HEBREWS 10:22–25

The eyes of the LORD are on those who fear him,
on those whose hope is in his unfailing love,

PSALM 33:18

Hope

No one whose hope is in you
    will ever be put to shame, O LORD.

PSALM 25:3

Be strong and take heart,
    all you who hope in the LORD.

PSALM 31:24

Find rest, O my soul, in God alone;
    my hope comes from him.
He alone is my rock and my salvation;
    he is my fortress, I will not be shaken.

PSALM 62:5–6

As for me, I will always have hope;
    I will praise you more and more, O LORD.

PSALM 71:14

I watch in hope for the LORD,
    I wait for God my Savior;
    my God will hear me.

MICAH 7:7

Hope

Blessed is he whose help is the God of Jacob,
> whose hope is in the LORD his God,
the Maker of heaven and earth,
> the sea, and everything in them—
> the LORD, who remains faithful forever.

PSALM 146:5–6

Wisdom is sweet to your soul;
> if you find it, there is a future hope for you,
> and your hope will not be cut off.

PROVERBS 24:14

Those who hope in the LORD
> will renew their strength.
They will soar on wings like eagles;
> they will run and not grow weary,
> they will walk and not be faint.

ISAIAH 40:31

Do the skies themselves send down showers?
No, it is you, O LORD our God.
> Therefore our hope is in you,
> for you are the one who does all this.

JEREMIAH 14:22

Hope

"For I know the plans I have for you," declares the LORD, "plans to prosper you and not to harm you, plans to give you hope and a future."

JEREMIAH 29:11

This I call to mind
>   and therefore I have hope:
Because of the LORD's great love we are not consumed,
>   for his compassions never fail.
They are new every morning;
>   great is your faithfulness.

LAMENTATIONS 3:21–23

We rejoice in the hope of the glory of God. Not only so, but we also rejoice in our sufferings, because we know that suffering produces perseverance; perseverance, character; and character, hope. And hope does not disappoint us, because God has poured out his love into our hearts by the Holy Spirit, whom he has given us.

ROMANS 5:2–5

Hope

I say to myself, "The LORD is my portion;
 therefore I will wait for him."
The LORD is good to those whose hope is in him,
 to the one who seeks him;
it is good to wait quietly
 for the salvation of the LORD.

LAMENTATIONS 3:24–26

For everything that was written in the past was written to teach us, so that through endurance and the encouragement of the Scriptures we might have hope.

ROMANS 15:4

May the God of hope fill you with all joy and peace as you trust in him, so that you may overflow with hope by the power of the Holy Spirit.

ROMANS 15:13

Hope

Luke 1:5-25

Zechariah and Elizabeth were without any children because she was barren. At that time in Israel, barrenness was considered a terrible disgrace. Together they most certainly agonized in prayer for a child. Now, at their advanced age, it could be assumed that all hope was lost. Though they might have given up hope for this prayer request, it is important to see that this couple never gave up faith in God. Verse 6 tells us that, regardless of this unanswered prayer, they were righteous before the Lord. God knew the desire of their hearts.

Our role as a couple is to bare our hearts before the Lord and trust that he knows best. His timing is perfect. His plans of us are better than we could ever have dreamed. Though this couple's wait was long, God eventually blessed them with an answer to their prayers that was greater than they could have dreamed or dare to ask for. They were selected to bring forth the child about whom the Lord himself would state: "Among those born of women there has not risen anyone greater than John the Baptist" (Matthew 11:11). This couple was blessed because their faith was in God, not in an answer to their prayer.

Marriage Devotional Bible

Joy

I will bless them and the places surrounding my hill.
I will send down showers in season; there will be
showers of blessing. The trees of the field will yield
their fruit and the ground will yield its crops; the
people will be secure in their land. They will know
that I am the LORD.

E Z E K I E L   3 4 : 2 6 – 2 7

To him who is able to keep you from falling and to
present you before his glorious presence without
fault and with great joy—to the only God our Savior
be glory, majesty, power and authority, through Jesus
Christ our Lord, before all ages, now and forever-
more!

J U D E   2 4 – 2 5

Though you have not seen Christ, you love him;
and even though you do not see him now, you
believe in him and are filled with an inexpressible
and glorious joy, for you are receiving the goal of
your faith, the salvation of your souls.

1   P E T E R   1 : 8

You have loved righteousness and hated wickedness;
  therefore God, your God,

Joy

has set you above your companions
by anointing you with the oil of joy.

HEBREWS 1:9

Your love has given me great joy and encouragement.

PHILEMON 7

The fruit of the Spirit is love, joy, peace, patience,
kindness, goodness, faithfulness, gentleness and self-
control.

GALATIANS 5:22–23

May the God of hope fill you with all joy and peace
as you trust in him, so that you may overflow with
hope by the power of the Holy Spirit.

ROMANS 15:13

We ... rejoice in God through our Lord Jesus
Christ, through whom we have now received recon-
ciliation.

ROMANS 5:11

Jesus said, "Until now you have not asked for anything in my name. Ask and you will receive, and

Joy

your joy will be complete."
JOHN 16:24

Be glad, O people of Zion,
    rejoice in the LORD your God,
for he has given you
    the autumn rains in righteousness.
He sends you abundant showers,
    both autumn and spring rains, as before.
The threshing floors will be filled with grain;
    the vats will overflow with new wine and oil.
"I will repay you for the years the locusts have
        eaten—
    the great locust and the young locust,
    the other locusts and the locust swarm—
my great army that I sent among you.
You will have plenty to eat, until you are full,
    and you will praise the name
    of the LORD your God,
    who has worked wonders for you;
never again will my people be shamed.
JOEL 2:23–26

Jesus said to his disciples, "Now is your time of grief,
but I will see you again and you will rejoice, and no

one will take away your joy."
JOHN 16:22

The LORD your God is with you,
    he is mighty to save.
He will take great delight in you,
    he will quiet you with his love,
    he will rejoice over you with singing.
ZEPHANIAH 3:17

When your words came, I ate them;
    they were my joy and my heart's delight,
for I bear your name,
    O LORD God Almighty.
JEREMIAH 15:16

As a mother comforts her child,
    so will I comfort you; ...
    When you see this, your heart will rejoice
    and you will flourish like grass.
ISAIAH 66:13–14

Joy

As a young man marries a maiden,
   so will your sons marry you;
as a bridegroom rejoices over his bride,
   so will your God rejoice over you.

ISAIAH 62:5

Our mouths were filled with laughter,
   our tongues with songs of joy.
Then it was said among the nations,
   "The LORD has done great things for them."
The LORD has done great things for us,
   and we are filled with joy.

PSALM 126:2–3

Let the rivers clap their hands,
   let the mountains sing together for joy.

PSALM 98:8

Light is shed upon the righteous
   and joy on the upright in heart.

PSALM 97:11

DEVOTIONAL THOUGHT ON
Joy

In marriage, as with any area of life, we can lose the perspective of where our blessings come from. Our perspective should always be one of deep gratitude to the giver of blessings. God has blessed us immeasurably just by giving us life. Our dissatisfaction or gratefulness depends on the perspective we choose.

One of our home videos of an earlier Christmas changed that perspective for us forever. As we watched our first Christmas with children, we were moved by two scenes. The first scene showed us to be overwhelmed with happiness and emotion over a used microwave I had purchased for Rosemary. In those days an inexpensive gift seemed to bring us so much joy. The real blessing, however, soon came crawling into the video scene. As we watched our then baby girl, we were overcome with the realization of how "rich" God had made us in the blessings that money can't buy.

When we take a blessing inventory now, we look at the things God has given that no amount of money could ever buy. We find that we are showered with blessings.

BOB AND ROSEMARY BARNES

Patience

The end of a matter is better than its beginning,
   and patience is better than pride.
Do not be quickly provoked in your spirit,
   for anger resides in the lap of fools.

ECCLESIASTES 7:8–9

Love is patient, love is kind. It does not envy, it does
not boast, it is not proud. It is not rude, it is not self-
seeking, it is not easily angered, It keeps no record of
wrongs ... but rejoices with the truth. It always protects, always trusts, always hopes, always perseveres.

1 CORINTHIANS 13:4–7

A patient man has great understanding.

PROVERBS 14:29

If we hope for what we do not yet have, we wait for
it patiently.

ROMANS 8:25

The fruit of the Spirit is love, joy, peace, patience,
kindness, goodness, faithfulness, gentleness and self-
control.

GALATIANS 5:22–23

Patience

Trust in the Lord and do good;
>dwell in the land and enjoy safe pasture.

Delight yourself in the LORD
>and he will give you the desires of your heart.

Commit your way to the LORD;
>trust in him and he will do this:

He will make your righteousness shine like the
dawn,
>the justice of your cause like the noonday sun.

Be still before the LORD and wait patiently for him.

PSALM 37:3–7

I waited patiently for the LORD;
>he turned to me and heard my cry. . . .

he set my feet on a rock
>and gave me a firm place to stand.

He put a new song in my mouth,
>a hymn of praise to our God.

Many will see and fear
>and put their trust in the LORD.

PSALM 40:1–3

Patience

If we are distressed, it is for your comfort and salvation; if we are comforted, it is for your comfort, which produces in you patient endurance of the same sufferings we suffer. And our hope for you is firm, because we know that just as you share in our sufferings, so also you share in our comfort.

2 CORINTHIANS 1:6–7

Be completely humble and gentle; be patient, bearing with one another in love.

EPHESIANS 4:2

As God's chosen people, holy and dearly loved, clothe yourselves with compassion, kindness, humility, gentleness and patience.

COLOSSIANS 3:12

Patience

NEHEMIAH 3

Rebuilding the walls of Jerusalem—what an immense task! It was a success because the Israelites worked together. One thing that doesn't appear to be part of this chapter is "complaining." The people seem so focused on doing their part that they aren't focused on their neighbor's responsibilities. They stand next to each other shoulder to shoulder, focusing only on their own sections. ...

There's a great principle here for the marriage relationship. Difficult tasks face each marriage. Some spouses have medical difficulties, while others have incredible parenting challenges. Serious financial difficulties seem to plague marriage relationships. Still other couples face a circumstance that has deflated trust in their marriage . Every marriage has a "wall " that has crumbled and needs to be rebuilt. ...

God reveals his amazing omniscience when we take the time to look at the spouse he has given us. Oftentimes one spouse will have the gifts to overcome the difficulty but not have the patience to endure. Yet it seems that God has linked that spouse, shoulder to shoulder, with a marriage partner who has that patience. Alone they would never able to complete the task that lies before them. But working together, as one flesh, they find that they can.

BOB AND ROSEMARY BARNES

Peace

The fruit of the Spirit is love, joy, peace, patience, kindness, goodness, faithfulness, gentleness and self-control.

GALATIANS 5:22–23

In Christ Jesus you who once were far away have been brought near. . . . For he himself is our peace, who has made the two one and has destroyed the barrier.

EPHESIANS 2:13–14

Let the peace of Christ rule in your hearts, since as members of one body you were called to peace. And be thankful.

COLOSSIANS 3:15

A heart at peace gives life to the body.

PROVERBS 14:30

The LORD gives strength to his people;
      the LORD blesses his people with peace.

PSALM 29:11

Peace

"My people will live in peaceful dwelling places,
    in secure homes,
in undisturbed places of rest," says the LORD.

ISAIAH 32:18

I will listen to what God the LORD will say;
    he promises peace to his people.

PSALM 85:8

You shall go out with joy
    and be led forth with peace;
the mountains and hills
    will burst into song before you,
and all the trees of the field
    will clap their hands.

ISAIAH 55:12

I will lie down and sleep in peace,
    for you alone, O LORD,
        make me dwell in safety.

PSALM 4:8

Make every effort to keep the unity of the Spirit
through the bond of peace.

EPHESIANS 4:3

GOD'S WORDS OF LIFE ON
Peace

The LORD bless you
    and keep you;
the LORD make his face shine upon you
    and be gracious to you;
the LORD turn his face toward you
    and give you peace.
NUMBERS 6:24–26

Love and faithfulness meet together;
    righteousness and peace kiss each other.
PSALM 85:10

Great peace have they who love your law,
    and nothing can make them stumble.
PSALM 119:165

Wisdom's ways are pleasant ways,
    and all her paths are peace.
PROVERBS 3:17

There is ... joy for those who promote peace.
PROVERBS 12:20

For to us a child is born,
    to us a son is given,
        and the government will be on his shoulders.

GOD'S WORDS OF LIFE ON
Peace

And he will be called
Wonderful Counselor, Mighty God,
Everlasting Father, Prince of Peace.

ISAIAH 9:6

You will keep in perfect peace
him whose mind is steadfast,
because he trusts in you, O LORD.

ISAIAH 26:3

When a man's ways are pleasing to the LORD,
he makes even his enemies live at peace with
him.

PROVERBS 16:7

The fruit of righteousness will be peace;
the effect of righteousness will be quietness
and confidence forever.

ISAIAH 32:17

LORD, you establish peace for us;
all that we have accomplished you have done
for us.

ISAIAH 26:12

GOD'S WORDS OF LIFE ON
Peace

Mercy, peace and love be yours in abundance.

JUDE 2

Peacemakers who sow in peace raise a harvest of righteousness.

JAMES 3:18

May the God of peace, who through the blood of the eternal covenant brought back from the dead our Lord Jesus, that great Shepherd of the sheep, equip you with everything good for doing his will, and may he work in us what is pleasing to him, through Jesus Christ, to whom be glory for ever and ever.

HEBREWS 13:20–21

Peace

PROVERBS 4:25–26

We recently celebrated a wedding anniversary in the mountains of Colorado. This was not a camping trip, however. We were going deluxe—a late morning brunch, a lazy afternoon by the pool, maybe a little window shopping and then a gourmet dinner. Well, that was the first day. When the second morning rolled around, we were ready for a change of pace. We wanted activity, an outdoor adventure. The night before, on our stroll through town, we had spotted a mountain bike rental shop. It was filled with dozens of bikes with fat, knobby tires for traversing rocky terrain. So after a quick breakfast, we bee-lined it for the bikes, mapped out a route and took off for the wilderness.

One thing we didn't consider, however, was the impact of the high altitude on our breathing. Add to that the steep inclines, muddy patches and crooked trails, and you can probably figure out that we did not get too far on our journey. We ended up returning to town and riding our bikes on paved, flat roads along the river. Ah, the serenity of a level path. No more huffing and puffing.

Proverbs has a lot to say about the benefits of traveling on a straight and level path. Of course, no marriage is exempt from a few steep inclines and some rocky terrain. They are a part of every marriage relationship. But generally speaking, we can do more than we think we can to smooth out the journey.

Proverbs speaks about "looking straight ahead" and "fixing our gaze." This is the talk of having a purpose, of having a mission. Have you ever written a purpose statement? More to the point, have you ever considered creating a mission statement unique to you as a married couple?

LES AND LESLIE PARROTT

Perseverance

We ... rejoice in our sufferings, because we know that suffering produces perseverance; perseverance, character; and character, hope. And hope does not disappoint us, because God has poured out his love into our hearts by the Holy Spirit, whom he has given us.

ROMANS 5:3–5

Make every effort to add to your faith goodness; and to goodness, knowledge; and to knowledge, self-control; and to self-control, perseverance; and to perseverance, godliness; and to godliness, brotherly kindness; and to brotherly kindness, love. For if you possess these qualities in increasing measure, they will keep you from being ineffective and unproductive in your knowledge of our Lord Jesus Christ.

2 PETER 1:5–8

Let love and faithfulness never leave you;
      bind them around your neck,
write them on the tables of your heart.
      Then you will win favor and a good name
in the sight of God and man.

PROVERBS 3:3–4

GOD'S WORDS OF LIFE ON
Perseverance

No temptation has seized you except what is common to man. And God is faithful; he will not let you be tempted beyond what you can bear. But when you are tempted, he will also provide a way out so that you can stand up under it.

1 CORINTHIANS 10:13

Jesus said, "I have told you these things, so that in me you may have peace. In this world you will have trouble. But take heart! I have overcome the world."

JOHN 16:33

Blessed is the man who perseveres under trial, because when he has stood the test, he will receive the crown of life that God has promised to those who love him.

JAMES 1:12

The righteous will flourish like a palm tree,
        they will grow like a cedar of Lebanon;
planted in the house of the LORD,
        they will flourish in the courts of our God.
They will still bear fruit in old age,
        they will stay fresh and green,
proclaiming, "The LORD is upright;
        he is my Rock."

PSALM 92:12–15

Perseverance

Those who trust in the LORD are like Mount Zion,
   which cannot be shaken but endures forever.

PSALM 125:1

We consider blessed those who have persevered. You
have heard of Job's perseverance and have seen what
the Lord finally brought about. The Lord is full of
compassion and mercy.

JAMES 5:11

Therefore, since we are surrounded by such a great
cloud of witnesses, let us throw off everything that
hinders and the sin that so easily entangles, and let
us run with perseverance the race marked out for us.
Let us fix our eyes on Jesus, the author and perfecter
of our faith, who for the joy set before him endured
the cross, scorning its shame, and sat down at the
right hand of the throne of God. Consider him who
endured such opposition from sinful men, so that
you will not grow weary and lose heart.

HEBREWS 12:1-3

Perseverance

The root system of most trees is as wide and deep as the leaf line is wide and high. That is not true, however, of the redwood, which has a shallow root system that spreads out in all directions. It is just not very deep. That fact of life creates a problem for a redwood standing alone. It can easily be blown over because the lack of deep roots gives it little stability. However, when two redwoods grow together, their root structures intertwine with each other and give one another strength. Though weak as separate trees, they become strong together. The same is true for spouses. "Two are better than one," said King Solomon.

Whether you live in one place for many years or relocate around the country according to job requirements, the most important roots you'll ever establish are in God and his Word. For this spiritual root system will bear much fruit. "I am the vine;" said Jesus, " ... apart from me you can do nothing ... If you remain in me and my words remain in you, ask whatever you wish, and it will be given you. This is to my Father's glory, that you bear much fruit, showing yourselves to be my disciples" (John 15:5–8).

As a couple grows together in their understanding of God and his Word, they become all the more "rooted and established in love" (Ephesians 3:17). Never forget that you as a couple, like the redwoods, become stronger together.

LES AND LESLIE PARROTT

Prayer

Jesus taught, "When you pray, go into your room, close the door and pray to your Father, who is unseen. Then your Father, who sees what is done in secret, will reward you. . . .

"This, then, is how you should pray: 'Our Father in heaven, hallowed be your name, your kingdom come, your will be done on earth as it is in heaven. Give us today our daily bread. Forgive us our debts, as we also have forgiven our debtors. And lead us not into temptation, but deliver us from the evil one.'"

MATTHEW 6:6, 9–13

"If my people, who are called by my name, will humble themselves and pray and seek my face and turn from their wicked ways, then will I hear from heaven and will forgive their sin," says the LORD.

2 CHRONICLES 7:14

Do not be anxious about anything, but in every-thing, by prayer and petition, with thanksgiving, present your requests to God. And the peace of God, which transcends all understanding, will guard your hearts and your minds in Christ Jesus.

PHILIPPIANS 4:6–7

Prayer

Jesus said, "For where two or three come together in my name, there am I with them."

MATTHEW 18:20

The Spirit helps us in our weakness. We do not know what we ought to pray for, but the Spirit himself intercedes for us with groans that words cannot express. And he who searches our hearts knows the mind of the Spirit, because the Spirit intercedes for the saints in accordance with God's will. And we know that in all things God works for the good of those who love him, who have been called according to his purpose.

ROMANS 8:26–28

Let us kneel
        before the LORD our Maker;
for he is our God
        and we are the people of his pasture,
the flock under his care.

PSALM 95:6–7

Let us then approach the throne of grace with confidence, so that we may receive mercy and find grace to help us in our time of need.

HEBREWS 4:16

Prayer

To you, O LORD, I lift up my soul;
  in you I trust, O my God.

PSALM 25:1-2

O LORD, I call to you; come quickly to me.
  Hear my voice when I call to you.
May my prayer be set before you like incense;
  may the lifting up of my hands be like the
  evening sacrifice.

PSALM 141:1-2

I thank my God every time I remember you. ... I
always pray with joy because of your partnership in
the gospel from the first day until now, being confi-
dent of this, that he who began a good work in you
will carry it on to completion until the day of Christ
Jesus. It is right for me to feel this way about all of
you, since I have you in my heart.

PHILIPPIANS 1:3-7

Confess your sins to each other and pray for each
other so that you may be healed.

JAMES 5:16

Prayer

When you stand praying, if you hold anything against anyone, forgive him, so that your Father in heaven may forgive you your sins.

MARK 11:25

I urge, then, first of all, that requests, prayers, intercession and thanksgiving be made for everyone—for kings and all those in authority, that we may live peaceful and quiet lives in all godliness and holiness. This is good, and pleases God our Savior, who wants all men to be saved and to come to a knowledge of the truth.

1 TIMOTHY 2:1–4

"You will call upon me and come and pray to me, and I will listen to you," declares the LORD.

JEREMIAH 29:12

The righteous cry out, and the LORD hears them;
        he delivers them from all their troubles.

PSALM 34:17

The LORD our God is near us whenever we pray to him.

DEUTERONOMY 4:7

Prayer

The angel Gabriel said to Daniel, "As soon as you began to pray, an answer was given, which I have come to tell you, for you are highly esteemed."

DANIEL 9:23

The LORD has heard my cry for mercy;
     the LORD accepts my prayer.

PSALM 6:9

Jesus said, "If you have faith as small as a mustard seed, you can say to this mountain, 'Move from here to there' and it will move. Nothing will be impossible for you."

MATTHEW 17:20

Prayer

HEBREWS 10:23–24

Claudia is more time-oriented than I am, so she is continually trying to "spur" me on. That comes naturally. But it's not so natural or easy to "spur one another on toward love and good deeds." Spouses greatly influence one another, and we need to use that influence in a positive way. One way we spur each other on toward love and good deeds is to pray faithfully for each other and with each other. This passage reminds us that God is faithful and will help us to hold unswervingly to the hope we profess. God fortifies a Christian marriage, and we can fortify our own marriage through prayer.

It hasn't always been easy for Claudia and me to pray together. At first we felt awkward and were hesitant to pray out loud. Someone suggested that we write down our prayer requests before we tried praying together. This really helped us resist sending messages to the other through prayer—like "God, please help her be a little more sensitive to my needs." Also, keeping a prayer journal over the years has helped us to grow in our faith as we see how God has answered our prayers—and not always in the way we wanted him to answer them—but always in our best interest.

DAVE AND CLAUDIA ARP

Pride

The meek will inherit the land
  and enjoy great peace.
PSALM 37:11

God guides the humble in what is right.
PSALM 25:9

When pride comes, then comes disgrace,
  but with humility comes wisdom.
PROVERBS 11:2

Pride only breeds quarrels,
  but wisdom is found in those who take advice.
PROVERBS 13:10

The LORD gives grace to the humble.
PROVERBS 3:34

Pride goes before destruction,
  a haughty spirit before a fall.
PROVERBS 16:18

God crowns the humble with salvation.
PSALM 149:4

Pride

A man's pride brings him low,
    but a man of lowly spirit gains honor.
PROVERBS 29:23

The end of a matter is better than its beginning,
    and patience is better than pride.
ECCLESIASTES 7:8

Each one should test his own actions. Then he can
take pride in himself, without comparing himself to
somebody else.
GALATIANS 6:4

The LORD sustains the humble.
PSALM 147:6

Be completely humble and gentle; be patient, bearing with one another in love.
EPHESIANS 4:2

Live in harmony with one another; be sympathetic,
love as brothers, be compassionate and humble.
1 PETER 3:8

GOD'S WORDS OF LIFE ON
Pride

All of you, clothe yourselves with humility toward one another, because, "God opposes the proud but gives grace to the humble." Humble yourselves, therefore, under God's mighty hand, that he may lift you up in due time.

1 PETER 5:5–6

An argument started among the disciples as to which of them would be the greatest. Jesus, knowing their thoughts, took a little child and had him stand beside him. Then he said to them, "Whoever welcomes this little child in my name welcomes me; and whoever welcomes me welcomes the one who sent me.

For he who is least among you all—he is the greatest."

LUKE 9:46–48

Devotional thought on
Pride

PROVERBS 11:2

"It's my way or the highway." Ever felt like that? If we are honest, we have all had times where we wanted something done our way while our spouse wanted it done another.

Make way for compromise—not one of my favorite words. I (Leslie) view it much the way I view such things as sit-ups and checkbook balancing: necessary but evil.

Some people start out marriage with the belief that they shouldn't have to negotiate because they should agree on everything. That's because during courtship they seem to agree on everything. But over time, different needs and issues are brought to bear. And if a husband and wife don't learn to eat a little humble pie and make some concessions now and then, they might as well give up. Marriage cannot survive without a little give and take.

Arriving at a mutually pleasing agreement doesn't just solve an immediate, specific problem; it ushers in a spirit of humility to the marriage. Selfish pride is the primary barrier to negotiating in marriage. No wonder Proverbs says that when pride enters the picture, it's a disgrace. But humility cultivates wisdom.

LES AND LESLIE PARROTT

Priorities

I have taken an oath and confirmed it,
> that I will follow your righteous laws, O LORD.

PSALM 119:106

Commit to the LORD whatever you do,
> and your plans will succeed.

PROVERBS 16:3

Trust in the LORD with all your heart
> and lean not on your own understanding;
in all your ways acknowledge him,
> and he will make your paths straight.

PROVERBS 3:5–6

The man who had received the five talents brought the other five. "Master," he said, "you entrusted me with five talents. See, I have gained five more. "His master replied, "Well done, good and faithful servant! You have been faithful with a few things; I will put you in charge of many things. Come and share your master's happiness!"

MATTHEW 25:20–21

Priorities

If anyone obeys his word, God's love is truly made complete in him. This is how we know we are in him: Whoever claims to live in him must walk as Jesus did.

1 JOHN 2:5-6

This is God's command: to believe in the name of his Son, Jesus Christ, and to love one another as he commanded us. Those who obey his commands live in him, and he in them. And this is how we know that he lives in us: We know it by the Spirit he gave us.

1 JOHN 3:23-24

My son, do not forget my teaching,
    but keep my commands in your heart,
for they will prolong your life many years
    and bring you prosperity.

PROVERBS 3:1-2

If the LORD delights in a man's way,
    he makes his steps firm;
though he stumble, he will not fall,
    for the LORD upholds him with his hand.

PSALM 37:23-24

Priorities

Whatever you do, work at it with all your heart, as working for the Lord, not for men, since you know that you will receive an inheritance from the Lord as a reward. It is the Lord Christ you are serving.

COLOSSIANS 3:23–24

Let us fix our eyes on Jesus, the author and perfecter of our faith, who for the joy set before him endured the cross, scorning its shame, and sat down at the right hand of the throne of God.

HEBREWS 12:2

Teach us to number our days aright,
  that we may gain a heart of wisdom.

PSALM 90:12

Devotional thought on

Priorities

GENESIS 13

The marriage relationship consists of a series of choices. The most significant choice is who you will serve with your marriage. Most married couples make this choice without thinking about it. Like Lot, they look around and see where many wonderful things abound, and then they pursue that direction. "Bigger" and "more" become the goals of their marriage.

In the early years of our marriage, this was a great conflict. I (Bob) felt the strong pull to focus all my energies on purchasing a home in the right neighborhood. Rosemary, on the other hand, believed that God would supply all our needs if we focused on him. It was a struggle in our marriage, until I realized that my preoccupation with the pursuit of things was futile. God had a better plan.

When Lot chose to move his life closer to the riches of the world, Abraham chose to serve only God. Abraham's total focus was pleasing to God. He knew that he could not serve both the things of the world and God.

The marriage team must make the same decision. Two masters cannot be served. The difficult decision must be made whether to serve God or serve things. The temptations dangling in front of each partner on the pages of catalogs and in advertisements can become very distracting. The decision of who or what our marriages will serve must be a daily choice and commitment.

There's nothing wrong with acquiring things. Abraham was a far wealthier person than Lot. Lot's mistake was that he focused too closely on the world … and failed. Abraham stayed focused on God … and prospered. The question to ask is, "What does our marriage serve? Does it serve God or does it serve the things of the world?"

BOB AND ROSEMARY BARNES

Resolving Conflict

If you have any encouragement from being united
with Christ, if any comfort from his love, if any fellowship with the Spirit, if any tenderness and compassion, then make my joy complete by being
like-minded, having the same love, being one in
spirit and purpose.

Do nothing out of selfish ambition or vain conceit,
but in humility consider others better than yourselves. Each of you should look not only to your
own interests, but also to the interests of others.

PHILIPPIANS 2:1–4

Let us not become weary in doing good, for at the
proper time we will reap a harvest if we do not give
up. therefore, as we have opportunity, let us do good
to all people, especially to those who belong to the
family of believers.

GALATIANS 6:9–10

Everyone should be quick to listen, slow to speak
and slow to become angry, for man's anger does not
bring about the righteous life that God desires.

JAMES 1:19–20

GOD'S WORDS OF LIFE ON
Resolving Conflict

Do not let the sun go down while you are still angry.
EPHESIANS 4:26

Love is patient, love is kind. It does not envy, it does not boast, it is not proud. It is not rude, it is not self-seeking, it is not easily angered, it keeps no record of wrongs. Love does not delight in evil but rejoices with the truth.
1 CORINTHIANS 13:4–6

A gentle answer turns away wrath,
    but a harsh word stirs up anger.
PROVERBS 15:1

Hatred stirs up dissension,
    but love covers over all wrongs.
PROVERBS 10:12

When words are many, sin is not absent,
    but he who holds his tongue is wise.
PROVERBS 10:19

A man of understanding holds his tongue.
PROVERBS 11:12

GOD'S WORDS OF LIFE ON
Resolving Conflict

A kindhearted woman gains respect. . . .
   A kind man benefits himself. . . .
PROVERBS 11:16

He who seeks good finds goodwill. . . .
PROVERBS 11:27

Reckless words pierce like a sword,
   but the tongue of the wise brings healing.
PROVERBS 12:18

He who guards his lips guards his life,
   but he who speaks rashly will come to ruin.
PROVERBS 13:3

DEVOTIONAL THOUGHT ON
Resolving Conflict

MATTHEW 18:19–20

"A family that prays together stays together" and "Prayer changes things" are two popular sayings. They may be cute and catchy, but they are also profoundly true. We learn from this passage that God does indeed hear and answer our prayers when we come to him.

Unfortunately, praying together as a couple can be very difficult. We are not just called to pray together; we must deal with the issues we are presenting to God, so that we can be in agreement on them.

Agreeing on a direction for your relationship, your family or in an area of conflict can be a huge hurdle. There have been times in our own marriage when it was hard to pray together about an issue because we disagreed so vehemently. One instance was when Rosemary and I had opposite opinions about whether or not to let one of our teenagers go to a party. It was hard to pray together because we each had our own ideas about what should be done. Difficult as it was, we stopped in the middle of the heat of the conflict and prayed. Doing this helped bring us back to our priorities.

Ironically, conflict offers an opportunity to strengthen marriage. When handled maturely, conflicts show us that we need to look to God for the answers. Then, as a team, we can present a unified petition to God—the only One who has all the right answers to begin with. At that point we will be drawing on that special strength when we join together in prayer as an agreeing, united force.

BOB AND ROSEMARY BARNES

Rest and Renewal

The beloved of the LORD rest secure in him.

DEUTERONOMY 33:12

My soul finds rest in God alone;
    my salvation comes from him.
He alone is my rock and my salvation;
    he is my fortress, I will never be shaken. . . .
Find rest, O my soul, in God alone;
    my hope comes from him.

PSALM 62:1–2, 5

This is what the Sovereign LORD, the Holy One of
Israel, says: In repentance and rest is your salvation,
in quietness and trust is your strength. . . .

ISAIAH 30:15

He who dwells in the shelter of the Most High
    will rest in the shadow of the Almighty.
I will say of the LORD, "He is my refuge and my
        fortress,
    my God, in whom I trust." . . .
He will cover you with his feathers,
    and under his wings you will find refuge;
    his faithfulness will be your shield and ram-
        part. . . .

Rest and Renewal

If you make the Most High your dwelling—
> even the LORD, who is my refuge—
then no harm will befall you. . . .

PSALM 91:1–2, 4, 9–10

My people will live in peaceful dwelling places,
> in secure homes,
> in undisturbed places of rest.

ISAIAH 32:18

The boundary lines have fallen for me in pleasant
> places;
> surely I have a delightful inheritance.
I will praise the LORD, who counsels me;
> even at night my heart instructs me.
I have set the LORD always before me.
> Because he is at my right hand, I will not be
> shaken.
Therefore my heart is glad and my tongue rejoices;
> my body also will rest secure, . . .
You have made known to me the path of life;
> you will fill me with joy in your presence,
with eternal pleasures at your right hand.

PSALM 16:6–9,11

Rest and Renewal

Jesus said, "Come to me, all you who are weary and burdened, and I will give you rest. Take my yoke upon you and learn from me, for I am gentle and humble in heart, and you will find rest for your souls."

MATTHEW 11:28–29

Stand at the crossroads and look;
    ask for the ancient paths,
ask where the good way is, and walk in it,
    and you will find rest for your souls.

JEREMIAH 6:16

Be at rest once more, O my soul,
    for the LORD has been good to you.

PSALM 116:7

Create in me a pure heart, O God,
    and renew a steadfast spirit within me.
Do not cast me from your presence
    or take your Holy Spirit from me.
Restore to me the joy of your salvation
    and grant me a willing spirit, to sustain me.

PSALM 51:10–12

Rest and Renewal

Praise the LORD, O my soul,
 and forget not all his benefits ...
who satisfies your desires with good things
 so that your youth is renewed like the eagle's.

PSALM 103:2, 5

The fear of the LORD leads to life:
 Then one rests content, untouched by trouble.

PROVERBS 19:23

Those who hope in the LORD
 will renew their strength.
They will soar on wings like eagles;
 they will run and not grow weary,
 they will walk and not be faint.

ISAIAH 40:31

Be transformed by the renewing of your mind. Then
you will be able to test and approve what God's will
is—his good, pleasing and perfect will.

ROMANS 12:2

Rest and Renewal

We do not lose heart. Though outwardly we are wasting away, yet inwardly we are being renewed day by day. For our light and momentary troubles are achieving for us an eternal glory that far outweighs them all. So we fix our eyes not on what is seen, but on what is unseen. For what is seen is temporary, but what is unseen is eternal.

2 CORINTHIANS 4:16–18

Because so many people were coming and going that [the disciples] did not even have a chance to eat, Jesus said to them, "Come with me by yourselves to a quiet place and get some rest."

MARK 6:31

When the kindness and love of God our Savior appeared, he saved us, not because of righteous things we had done, but because of his mercy. He saved us through the washing of rebirth and renewal by the Holy Spirit, whom he poured out on us generously through Jesus Christ our Savior, so that, having been justified by his grace, we might become heirs having the hope of eternal life.

TITUS 3:4–7

DEVOTIONAL THOUGHT ON
Rest and Renewal

SONG OF SONGS 1:16–17

In most homes the last room to get special attention is the master bedroom. It's the last place a visitor will ever see, so it's often the last place a couple decorates or cleans up. The living room gets a beautiful painting on the wall, but the bedroom is often the place where the laundry gets dumped for eventual folding.

This passage in Song of Songs gives us a visual picture of a marital sanctuary. Two lovers are walking outdoors, imagining that the "green field" is their bed and the "cedar trees" above are the beams of their house.

With hectic schedules and a myriad of children's activities to go to, is there a place like this in your marriage where you can find peace, tranquility and relationship? Perhaps the bedroom should become just that place. Instead of a place to sleep, it can become a place to grow deeper in love.

So spend a few moments together each day sitting in that "wooded forest" of your sanctuary. It's not just a purchase of the right furniture or tranquil paintings that will transform the master bedroom into a sanctuary. Each couple must devote time for each other—listening, sharing, loving and praying. Take time together to sit in the "cedar forest" of your bedroom.

BOB AND ROSEMARY BARNES

Romance

Husbands ought to love their wives as their own bodies. He who loves his wife loves himself.

EPHESIANS 5:28

I found the one my heart loves.
I held him and would not let him go.

SONG OF SONGS 3:4

Go, eat your food with gladness, and drink your wine with a joyful heart, for it is now that God favors what you do. Always be clothed in white, and always anoint your head with oil. Enjoy life with your wife, whom you love.

ECCLESIASTES 9:7–9

Turn your eyes from me; they overwhelm me. . . .
Who is this that appears like the dawn,
fair as the moon, bright as the sun,
majestic as the stars in procession?

SONG OF SONGS 6:5, 10

Let love and faithfulness never leave you . . .
write them on the tablet of your heart.

PROVERBS 3:3

My lover spoke and said to me,

Romance

Arise, my darling,
   my beautiful one, and come with me.
See! The winter is past;
   the rains are over and gone.
Flowers appear on the earth;
   the season of singing has come.
SONG OF SONGS 2:10–12

A longing fulfilled is sweet to the soul.
PROVERBS 13:19

Arise, come, my darling;
   my beautiful one, come with me.
My dove in the clefts of the rock,
   in the hiding places on the mountainside,
show me your face,
   let me hear your voice;
for your voice is sweet,
   and your face is lovely.
Catch for us the foxes,
   the little foxes
that ruin the vineyards,
   our vineyards that are in bloom.
My lover is mine and I am his.
SONG OF SONGS 2:13–16

Romance

His banner over me is love.

SONG OF SONGS 2:4

Place me like a seal over your heart,
    like a seal on your arm;
for love is as strong as death,
    its jealousy unyielding as the grave.
It burns like blazing fire,
    like a mighty flame.
Many waters cannot quench love;
    rivers cannot wash it away.
If one were to give
    all the wealth of his house for love,
    it would be utterly scorned.

SONG OF SONGS 8:6–7

Let him kiss me with the kisses of his mouth—
    for your love is more delightful than wine.

SONG OF SONGS 1:2

Romance

The LORD God said, "It is not good for the man to be alone. I will make a helper suitable for him." Now the LORD God had formed out of the ground all the beasts of the field and all the birds of the air. He brought them to the man to see what he would name them; and whatever the man called each living creature, that was its name. So the man gave names to all the livestock, the birds of the air and all the beasts of the field. But for Adam no suitable helper was found.

So the LORD God caused the man to fall into a deep sleep; and while he was sleeping, he took one of the man's ribs and closed up the place with flesh.

Then the LORD God made a woman from the rib he had taken out of the man, and he brought her to the man.

The man said, "This is now bone of my bones and flesh of my flesh; she shall be called 'woman,' for she was taken out of man."

For this reason a man will leave his father and mother and be united to his wife, and they will become one flesh.

GENESIS 2:18–24

Romance

Above all, love each other deeply, because love covers over a multitude of sins.

1 PETER 4:8

You have stolen my heart, my sister, my bride;
    you have stolen my heart
with one glance of your eyes,
    with one jewel of your necklace.
How delightful is your love, my sister, my bride!
    How much more pleasing is your love than
    wine,
    and the fragrance of your perfume than any
    spice!

SONG OF SONGS 4:9–10

Romance

1 PETER 4:8

It was our one-year anniversary—June 30, 1985. Whew! A whole year of being married. Just how would we commemorate this important milestone? A romantic dinner and a walk under the stars? Nope. We packed a picnic lunch with tuna fish sandwiches and diet pop and drove up the coast to Santa Barbara, three or so hours away. It was Les's idea. Okay, I thought. This could be fun. We'll have time to talk as we drive, and we can eat our lunch on the beach. But Les, now in graduate school, had a different idea. He was one week into a stressful summer school course, taking Greek, so he brought along a taped lecture to listen to on our drive and a pack of flash cards to study for his next exam.

So much for romance, at least on that day. I shouldn't paint an incorrect picture—Les can be very romantic. On my birthday this year, for example, he took me to the swankiest restaurant in town and had prearranged with the maitre d' to have a gift delivered to our table with my favorite dessert.

Still, in our home, romance can be a hit or miss endeavor. Of course, I do my part. Like the time I planned a weekend getaway as a surprise for Les. That was when I learned he doesn't think surprises are very romantic! Or the time I thought he would enjoy going to a theater production instead of skiing with his friends. He didn't.

Well, in case you haven't already guessed, we haven't discovered the one secret to romance in marriage. ... But we have discovered that a big part of cultivating romance is learning to love each other in spite of expectations that aren't met. That's a lesson couples can learn from Peter when he writes, " ... love each other deeply, because love covers over a multitude of sins."

LES AND LESLIE PARROTT

Serving

Serve wholeheartedly, as if you were serving the Lord, not men, because you know that the Lord will reward everyone for whatever good he does, whether he is slave or free.

EPHESIANS 6:7–8

Whatever you do, work at it with all your heart, as working for the Lord, not for men, since you now that you will receive an inheritance from the Lord as a reward. It is the Lord Christ you are serving.

COLOSSIANS 3:23–24

Jesus said to them, "The kings of the Gentiles lord it over them; and those who exercise authority over them call themselves Benefactors. But you are not to be like that. Instead, the greatest among you should be like the youngest, and the one who rules like the one who serves. For who is greater, the one who is at the table or the one who serves? Is it not the one who is at the table? But I am among you as one who serves."

LUKE 22:25–27

Serving

Your attitude should be the same as that of Christ
Jesus:
Who, being in very nature God,
> did not consider equality with God something
> to be grasped,
but made himself nothing,
> taking the very nature of a servant,
> being made in human likeness.
And being found in appearance as a man,
> he humbled himself
> and became obedient to death—
>> even death on a cross!
Therefore God exalted him to the highest place
> and gave him the name that is above every
> name,
that at the name of Jesus every knee should bow,
> in heaven and on earth and under the earth,
and every tongue confess that Jesus Christ is Lord,
> to the glory of God the Father.

PHILIPPIANS 2:5–11

Serving

There are different kinds of gifts, but the same Spirit. There are different kinds of service, but the same Lord. There are different kinds of working, but the same God works all of them in all men. Now to each one the manifestation of the Spirit is given for the common good. To one there is given through the Spirit the message of wisdom, to another the message of knowledge by means of the same Spirit, to another faith by the same Spirit, to another gifts of healing by that one Spirit, ... All these are the work of one and the same Spirit, and he gives them to each one, just as he determines.

1 CORINTHIANS 12:4–11

Serving

MARK 14:1–9

Love is not simply fulfilling marital responsibility. It is meant to go far beyond relational duty. Love has no boundaries of excess. It persists unconditionally. It is an outpouring of extravagant, sacrificial love.

To lavish love on one's spouse is to choose to do things that are beyond need or duty. For instance, Bob is very frugal. And he likes staying in his comfort zone. That means when we travel, his choice would be to stay in the same kind of inexpensive motel each night. But we don't. He does something that is way out of his comfort zone. When we travel, which we do frequently, Bob does some homework and makes reservations for us to stay at bed and breakfasts. Why does he do it? Why does he step way out of his comfort zone and spend the extra money? He does it only to lavish me with love.

Going beyond the ordinary expected actions shows incredible "Christ-like love" for our spouse—an expression of love so extraordinary that it cannot possibly go unnoticed. Extravagant love can only be motivated by a desire to please Christ. The woman with the alabaster jar found her expression of lavished love. The quest for each of us as spouses is to find ours.

BOB AND ROSEMARY BARNES

GOD'S WORDS OF LIFE ON
Spiritual Growth

Being strengthened with all power according to his glorious might so that you may have great endurance and patience, and joyfully giving thanks to the Father, who has qualified you to share in the inheritance of the saints in the kingdom of light.

COLOSSIANS 1:11–12

We do not lose heart. Though outwardly we are wasting away, yet inwardly we are being renewed day by day.

2 CORINTHIANS 4:16

Since we belong to the day, let us be self-controlled, putting on faith and love as a breastplate, and the hope of salvation as a helmet. For God did not appoint us to suffer wrath but to receive salvation through our Lord Jesus Christ. He died for us so that, whether we are awake or asleep, we may live together with him. Therefore encourage one another and build each other up, just as in fact you are doing.

1 THESSALONIANS 5:8–11

Those who trust in the LORD are like Mount Zion,
        which cannot be shaken but endures forever.

Spiritual Growth

As the mountains surround Jerusalem,
    so the LORD surrounds his people
    both now and forevermore.
PSALM 125:1-2

In the LORD alone are righteousness and strength.
ISAIAH 45:24

Thanks be to God! He gives us the victory through
our Lord Jesus Christ. Therefore, ... stand firm. Let
nothing move you. Always give yourselves fully to
the work of the Lord, because you know that your
labor in the Lord is not in vain.
1 CORINTHIANS 15:57-58

Therefore, since we are surrounded by such a great
cloud of witnesses, let us throw off everything that
hinders and the sin that so easily entangles, and let
us run with perseverance the race marked out for us.
Let us fix our eyes on Jesus, the author and perfecter
of our faith, who for the joy set before him endured
the cross, scorning its shame, and sat down at the
right hand of the throne of God. Consider him who
endured such opposition from sinful men, so that
you will not grow weary and lose heart.
HEBREWS 12:1-3

Spiritual Growth

Keep on loving each other as brothers. Do not forget to entertain strangers, for by so doing some people have entertained angels without knowing it. Remember those in prison as if you were their fellow prisoners, and those who are mistreated as if you yourselves were suffering.

HEBREWS 13:1–3

So then, just as you received Christ Jesus as Lord, continue to live in him, rooted and built up in him, strengthened in the faith as you were taught, and overflowing with thankfulness.

COLOSSIANS 2:6–7

Against all hope, Abraham in hope believed and so became the father of many nations, just as it had been said to him, "So shall your offspring be." Without weakening in his faith, he faced the fact that his body was as good as dead—since he was about a hundred years old—and that Sarah's womb was also dead. Yet he did not waver through unbelief regarding the promise of God, but was strengthened in his faith and gave glory to God, being fully persuaded that God had power to do what he had promised. This is why "it was credited to him as righteous-

Spiritual Growth

ness." The words "it was credited to him" were written not for him alone, but also for us, to whom God will credit righteousness—for us who believe in him who raised Jesus our Lord from the dead.

ROMANS 4:18–24

Like newborn babies, crave pure spiritual milk, so that by it you may grow up in your salvation, now that you have tasted that the Lord is good.

1 PETER 2:2–3

It was God who gave some to be apostles, some to be prophets, some to be evangelists, and some to be pastors and teachers, to prepare God's people for works of service, so that the body of Christ may be built up until we all reach unity in the faith and in the knowledge of the Son of God and become mature, attaining to the whole measure of the fullness of Christ.

Then we will no longer be infants, tossed back and forth by the waves, and blown here and there by every wind of teaching and by the cunning and craftiness of men in their deceitful scheming. Instead, speaking the truth in love, we will in all things grow up into him who is the Head, that is, Christ.

Spiritual Growth

From him the whole body, joined and held together by every supporting ligament, grows and builds itself up in love, as each part does its work.

EPHESIANS 4:11–16

Jesus says, "Here I am! I stand at the door and knock. If anyone hears my voice and opens the door, I will come in and eat with him, and he with me."

REVELATION 3:20

Spiritual Growth

REVELATION 3:20

This verse is often used and even quoted in reference to inviting Jesus Christ into your life as Lord and Savior. It also teaches a wonderful lesson about enjoying his fellowship. The concept of dining with the Lord would certainly imply that. The Lord wants to have fellowship with us and desires for us to open up to him. ...

Unfortunately, in the fast pace of life, we can forget the most important one in our lives. We can overlook the joy of communicating with the Creator and making him a part of our day. Not only should we individually "dine" with him, but what a blessing in our marriage to fellowship with our divine "guest" together as a couple!

Sharing Scripture or ideas as a couple that we have learned from our own personal study is a wonderful way to fellowship with God together. Making him a part of our decision-making process, through prayer, is another way to fellowship together with Christ. ...

Through fellowship with Jesus, we welcome Jesus' life-changing presence and power into our daily walk. Let us always open the door of our lives to him.

BOB AND ROSEMARY BARNES

Strength

The LORD is my strength and my song;
    he has become my salvation.
He is my God, and I will praise him,
    my father's God, and I will exalt him.

EXODUS 15:2

Be strong and courageous. Do not be terrified; do
not be discouraged, for the LORD your God will be
with you wherever you go.

JOSHUA 1:9

Wealth and honor come from you, LORD;
    you are the ruler of all things.
In your hands are strength and power
    to exalt and give strength to all.
Now, our God, we give you thanks,
    and praise your glorious name.

1 CHRONICLES 29:12–13

In your unfailing love you will lead
    the people you have redeemed, O LORD.
In your strength you will guide them
    to your holy dwelling.

EXODUS 15:13

Strength

For the eyes of the LORD range throughout the earth to strengthen those whose hearts are fully committed to him.

2 CHRONICLES 16:9

Look to the LORD and his strength;
   seek his face always.

1 CHRONICLES 16:11

The joy of the LORD is your strength.

NEHEMIAH 8:10

It is God who arms me with strength
   and makes my way perfect.
He makes my feet like the feet of a deer;
   he enables me to stand on the heights.

PSALM 18:32–33

The LORD is my strength and my shield;
   my heart trusts in him, and I am helped.
My heart leaps for joy
   and I will give thanks to him in song.
The LORD is the strength of his people,
   a fortress of salvation for his anointed one.

PSALM 28:7–8

Strength

The LORD gives strength to his people;
    the LORD blesses his people with peace.

PSALM 29:11

God is our refuge and strength,
    an ever-present help in trouble.
Therefore we will not fear, though the earth give way
    and the mountains fall into
    the heart of the sea,
though its waters roar and foam
    and the mountains quake with their surging.

PSALM 46:1–3

The Lord is faithful, and he will strengthen and protect you from the evil one.

2 THESSALONIANS 3:3

I can do everything through Christ who gives me strength.

PHILIPPIANS 4:13

Strength

EXODUS 5

Working conditions in Pharaoh's brick factory were already horrendous. Then he mandated that the Israelite brick makers gather their own straw. With the same required quota of bricks, getting enough straw became a huge problem. But they couldn't just decide not to use straw because the bricks wouldn't hold together; straw gives bricks texture and strength.

Taking this analogy and applying it to your relationship, ask yourself what is "the straw" in your marriage—what provides its texture and strength? The problems or obstacles you must overcome can actually be positive if you face them together. . . .

What problems are you facing in your marriage? If you can look at them as "straw" rather than as problems, then together you can overcome them and strengthen your relationship. Remember that the Israelites were not alone in their problems. You may not have Moses and Aaron to represent you, but you do have God Almighty, who wants to empower your marriage and make it a model for others to follow.

DAVE AND CLAUDIA ARP

GOD'S WORDS OF LIFE ON
Thankfulness

Give thanks to the LORD, call on his name;
  make known among the nations
  what he has done.

1 CHRONICLES 16:8

Praise the LORD.
I will extol the LORD with all my heart
  in the council of the upright
  and in the assembly.
Great are the works of the LORD;
  they are pondered by all who delight in them.

PSALM 111:1–2

Give thanks to the LORD, for he is good;
  his love endures forever.
Let Israel say:
  "His love endures forever."
Let the house of Aaron say:
  "His love endures forever."
Let those who fear the LORD say:
  "His love endures forever."

PSALM 118:1–4

My heart leaps with joy
  and I will give thanks to the LORD in song.

PSALM 28:7

GOD'S WORDS OF LIFE ON
Thankfulness

Enter the LORD's gates with thanksgiving
    and his courts with praise;
give thanks to him and praise his name.
PSALM 100:4

Every good and perfect gift is from above, coming
down from the Father of the heavenly lights, who
does not change like shifting shadows.
JAMES 1:17

Since we are receiving a kingdom that cannot be
shaken, let us be thankful, and so worship God
acceptably with reverence and awe.
HEBREWS 12:28

Everything God created is good, and nothing is to
be rejected if it is received with thanksgiving.
1 TIMOTHY 4:4

Through Jesus, therefore, let us continually offer to
God a sacrifice of praise—the fruit of lips that con-
fess his name.
HEBREWS 13:15

Thankfulness

The LORD your God will bless you in all your harvest and in all the work of your hands, and your joy will be complete.

DEUTERONOMY 16:15

Praise the LORD, O my soul,
      and forget not all his benefits—
who forgives all your sins
      and heals all your diseases,
who redeems your life from the pit
      and crowns you with love and compassion,
who satisfies your desires with good things
      so that your youth is renewed like the eagle's.

PSALM 103:2–5

Our mouths were filled with laughter,
      our tongues with songs of joy.
Then it was said among the nations,
      "The LORD has done great things for them."
The LORD has done great things for us,
      and we are filled with joy.

PSALM 126:2–3

I have learned to be content whatever the circumstances. I know what it is to be in need, and I know

Thankfulness

what it is to have plenty. I have learned the secret of being content in any and every situation. ... I can do everything through Christ who gives me strength.

PHILIPPIANS 4:11–13

Thanks be to God! He gives us the victory through our Lord Jesus Christ.

1 CORINTHIANS 15:57

Surely God is my salvation;
    I will trust and not be afraid.
The LORD, the LORD, is my strength and my song;
    he has become my salvation."
With joy you will draw water
    from the wells of salvation.
In that day you will say:
    "Give thanks to the LORD, call on his name;
    make known among the nations
    what he has done,
    and proclaim that his name is exalted.
Sing to the LORD, for he has done glorious things;
    let this be known to all the world.
Shout aloud and sing for joy, people of Zion,
    for great is the Holy One of Israel among you."

ISAIAH 12:2–6

Thankfulness

Be joyful always; pray continually; give thanks in all circumstances, for this is God's will for you in Christ Jesus.

1 THESSALONIANS 5:16–18

Let the peace of Christ rule in your hearts, since as members of one body you were called to peace. And be thankful.

COLOSSIANS 3:15

Just as you received Christ Jesus as Lord, continue to live in him, rooted and built up in him, strengthened in the faith as you were taught, and overflowing with thankfulness.

COLOSSIANS 2:6–7

DEVOTIONAL THOUGHT ON
Thankfulness

ISAIAH 12:4

Isaiah reminds us, "Give thanks to the LORD, call on his name; make known among the nations what he has done." What a great verse to apply to marriage. We hear so much negative news, publicizing the positive can be a breath of fresh air in the stale world of reality. We can start by thanking God for our spouse, our family, our health, for shelter, clothing and food.

During the years we lived in Vienna, Austria, Thanksgiving Day was not a national holiday. We didn't have extended family close by, but we built our own holiday traditions. One Thanksgiving in Vienna stands out as a time we realized how good God is. A pastor from Romania had joined us for the holiday. At that time, Christians in Romania experienced persecution and very hard times. Food was scarce there. Things we take for granted, like plenty of heat, hot water and warm clothes, were luxuries to them. Our guest had few worldly possessions and many concerns, but he radiated a spirit of thankfulness. We felt God's presence in a special way on that Thanksgiving.

Pause with us and thank God for all the ways he has blessed you, your marriage and your family. Then tell others.

DAVE AND CLAUDIA ARP

True Love

Husbands, love your wives, just as Christ loved the church and gave himself up for her to make her holy, cleansing her by the washing with water through the word, and to present her to himself as a radiant church, without stain or wrinkle or any other blemish, but holy and blameless. In this same way, husbands ought to love their wives as their own bodies. He who loves his wife loves himself. After all, no one ever hated his own body, but he feeds and cares for it, just as Christ does the church—for we are members of his body. "For this reason a man will leave his father and mother and be united to his wife, and the two will become one flesh." This is a profound mystery—but I am talking about Christ and the church.

EPHESIANS 5:25–32

Love is patient, love is kind. ... It always protects, always trusts, always hopes, always perseveres. Love never fails. But where there are prophecies, they will cease; where there are tongues, they will be stilled; where there is knowledge, it will pass away. For we know in part and we prophesy in part, but when perfection comes, the imperfect disappears.

1 CORINTHIANS 13:4, 7–10

True Love

To Christ who loves us and has freed us from our sins by his blood, and has made us to be a kingdom and priests to serve his God and Father—to him be glory and power for ever and ever!

REVELATION 1:5–6

How great is the love the Father has lavished on us, that we should be called children of God! And that is what we are!

1 JOHN 3:1

This is how we know what love is: Jesus Christ laid down his life for us. And we ought to lay down our lives for our brothers.

1 JOHN 3:16

There is no fear in love. But perfect love drives out fear. . . .

1 JOHN 4:18

We love because God first loved us.

1 JOHN 4:19

Above all, love each other deeply, because love covers over a multitude of sins.

1 PETER 4:8

GOD'S WORDS OF LIFE ON
True Love

Love one another deeply, from the heart.

1 PETER 1:22

When the kindness and love of God our Savior
appeared, he saved us, not because of righteous
things we had done, but because of his mercy. He
saved us through the washing of rebirth and renewal
by the Holy Spirit, whom he poured out on us generously through Jesus Christ our Savior, so that, having been justified by his grace, we might become
heirs having the hope of eternal life.

TITUS 3:4–7

May the Lord make your love increase and overflow
for each other and for everyone else, just as ours does
for you.

1 THESSALONIANS 3:12

This is my prayer: that your love may abound more
and more in knowledge and depth of insight, so that
you may be able to discern what is best and may be
pure and blameless until the day of Christ, filled
with the fruit of righteousness that comes through
Jesus Christ—to the glory and praise of God.

PHILIPPIANS 1:9–11

True Love

Be imitators of God, therefore, as dearly loved children and live a life of love, just as Christ loved us and gave himself up for us as a fragrant offering and sacrifice to God.

EPHESIANS 5:1–2

I pray that out of his glorious riches he may strengthen you with power through his Spirit in your inner being, so that Christ may dwell in your hearts through faith. And I pray that you, being rooted and established in love, may have power, together with all the saints, to grasp how wide and long and high and deep is the love of Christ, and to know this love that surpasses knowledge—that you may be filled to the measure of all the fullness of God.

EPHESIANS 3:16–19

Dear friends, let us love one another, for love comes from God. Everyone who loves has been born of God and knows God. Whoever does not love does not know God, because God is love. This is how God showed his love among us: He sent his one and only Son into the world that we might live through him. This is love: not that we loved God, but that he loved us and sent his Son as an atoning sacrifice for

True Love

our sins. Dear friends, since God so loved us, we also ought to love one another. No one has ever seen God; but if we love one another, God lives in us and his love is made complete in us. We know that we live in him and he in us, because he has given us of his Spirit. And we have seen and testify that the Father has sent his Son to be the Savior of the world. If anyone acknowledges that Jesus is the Son of God, God lives in him and he in God.

And so we know and rely on the love God has for us. God is love. Whoever lives in love lives in God, and God in him.

1 JOHN 4:7–16

True Love

PSALM 23

During the first year of our marriage, a marriage book uncovered a secret neither of us wanted to face. It showed us how we were each counting on the other person to make us feel significant. At a subconscious level, I (Les) was saying, "I need to feel important. I expect you to meet that need by respecting me no matter how I behave and by supporting me in whatever I choose to do. I want you to treat me as the most important person in the world. My goal in marrying you was to find my significance through you." Leslie had a similar unconscious message: "I have never felt as deeply loved as my nature requires. I am expecting you to meet that need through gentle affection even when I'm in a bad mood or not being sensitive to what you need. Don't let me down."

This was hard to swallow, but it was true. We each desperately wanted the other person to meet our need for significance, even though this was an unrealistic expectation for any person.

So are we stuck, forever floundering between fleeting moments of relational fulfillment?

Fortunately not. While our earthly relationships will let us down time and again, our relationship with God can genuinely and fully meet our deepest need for significance. And Psalm 23 stands as a poetic reminder to every married person that, no matter how difficult loving your spouse can be, you can rely on the Lord as your Shepherd to restore our soul, comfort you and meet your deepest needs.

LES AND LESLIE PARROTT

Trust

You will keep in perfect peace
    him whose mind is steadfast,
    because he trusts in you.
Trust in the LORD forever,
    for the LORD, the LORD, is the Rock eternal.
ISAIAH 26:3–4

LORD, you establish peace for us;
    all that we have accomplished you have done
    for us.
ISAIAH 26:12

Trust in the LORD with all your heart
    and lean not on your own understanding;
in all your ways acknowledge him,
    and he will make your paths straight.
PROVERBS 3:5–6

Offer right sacrifices
    and trust in the LORD.
Many are asking, "Who can show us any good?"
    Let the light of your face shine upon us, O
    LORD.
You have filled my heart with greater joy
    than when their grain and new wine abound.

GOD'S WORDS OF LIFE ON
Trust

I will lie down and sleep in peace,
for you alone, O LORD,
make me dwell in safety.

PSALM 4:5–8

O LORD, you have searched me
and you know me.
You know when I sit and when I rise;
you perceive my thoughts from afar.
You discern my going out and my lying down;
you are familiar with all my ways.
Before a word is on my tongue
you know it completely, O LORD.
You hem me in behind and before;
you have laid your hand upon me.
Such knowledge is too wonderful for me,
too lofty for me to attain.
Where can I go from your Spirit?
Where can I flee from your presence?
If I go up to the heavens, you are there;
if I make my bed in the depths, you are there.
If I rise on the wings of the dawn,
if I settle on the far side of the sea,
even there your hand will guide me,
your right hand will hold me fast.

PSALM 139:1–10

GOD'S WORDS OF LIFE ON
Trust

I trust in your unfailing love;
>   my heart rejoices in your salvation.
I will sing to the LORD,
>   for he has been good to me.

PSALM 13:5–6

Some trust in chariots and some in horses,
>   but we trust in the name of the LORD our God.

PSALM 20:7

The LORD is my strength and my shield;
>   my heart trusts in him, and I am helped.
My heart leaps for joy
>   and I will give thanks to him in song.

PSALM 28:7

The LORD's unfailing love
>   surrounds the man who trusts in him.

PSALM 32:10

Commit your way to the LORD;
>   trust in him and he will do this:
He will make your righteousness shine
>   like the dawn,
>   the justice of your cause like the noonday sun.

PSALM 37:5–6

GOD'S WORDS OF LIFE ON
Trust

Blessed is the man
who makes the LORD his trust.

PSALM 40:4

"See, I lay a stone in Zion,
a chosen and precious cornerstone,
and the one who trusts in him
will never be put to shame," says the Lord.

1 PETER 2:6

I know whom I have believed, and am convinced
that God is able to guard what I have entrusted to
him for that day.

2 TIMOTHY 1:12

May the God of hope fill you with all joy and peace
as you trust in him, so that you may overflow with
hope by the power of the Holy Spirit.

ROMANS 15:13

Jesus said, "Do not let your hearts be troubled. Trust
in God; trust also in me."

JOHN 14:1

GOD'S WORDS OF LIFE ON
Trust

The LORD is good,
> a refuge in times of trouble.
He cares for those who trust in him.

NAHUM 1:7

Blessed is the man who trusts in the LORD,
> whose confidence is in him.
He will be like a tree planted by the water
> that sends out its roots by the stream.
It does not fear when heat comes;
> its leaves are always green.
It has no worries in a year of drought
> and never fails to bear fruit.

JEREMIAH 17:7–8

This is what the Sovereign LORD,
> the Holy One of Israel, says:
> > "In repentance and rest is your salvation,
> > in quietness and trust is your strength."...

ISAIAH 30:15

Trust

GENESIS 50

Joseph grew up in a wealthy family where his doting father met his needs. Then one day, to his shock, he lost it all. Joseph's jealous brothers sold him into slavery. In one moment Joseph lost his things and his family.

During that long journey to Egypt, Joseph had to decide who or what he trusted. In good circumstances and in bad, where did he place his trust? Perhaps if it weren't for the difficult circumstances in that foreign land, Joseph would never have learned that he must focus on trusting God and God alone. Even though life came crashing down, Joseph knew he could trust God (see verse 20).

Who or what do you put your trust in? Some put their trust in things. Others put their trust in people. But things will be gone in a flash. And people will inevitably disappoint us. If our happiness comes from things and people, we are vulnerable to misery.

Even a marriage can't be the ultimate place to look for security and happiness. That's too much pressure to put on a marriage. Happiness and security must come from something that can never leave or forsake a person.

BOB AND ROSEMARY BARNES

Unity

May the God who gives endurance and encouragement give you a spirit of unity among yourselves as
you follow Christ Jesus, so that with one heart and
mouth you may glorify the God and Father of our
Lord Jesus Christ. Accept one another, then, just as
Christ accepted you, in order to bring praise to God.

ROMANS 15:5–7

Make every effort to keep the unity of the Spirit
through the bond of peace. There is one body and
one Spirit—just as you were called to one hope
when you were called—one Lord, one faith, one
baptism; one God and Father of all, who is over all
and through all and in all.

EPHESIANS 4:3–5

As God's chosen people, holy and dearly loved,
clothe yourselves with compassion, kindness, humility, gentleness and patience. Bear with each other and
forgive whatever grievances you may have against one
another. Forgive as the Lord forgave you. And over all
these virtues put on love, which binds them all
together in perfect unity. Let the peace of Christ rule
in your hearts, since as members of one body you
were called to peace. And be thankful.

COLOSSIANS 3:12–15

GOD'S WORDS OF LIFE ON
Unity

Jesus prayed, "My prayer is not for [my disciples] alone. I pray also for those who will believe in me through their message, that all of them may be one, Father, just as you are in me and I am in you. May they also be in us so that the world may believe that you have sent me. I have given them the glory that you gave me, that they may be one as we are one: I in them and you in me. May they be brought to complete unity to let the world know that you sent me and have loved them even as you have loved me."

JOHN 17:20–23

I appeal to you, ... in the name of our Lord Jesus Christ, that all of you agree with one another so that there may be no divisions among you and that you may be perfectly united in mind and thought.

1 CORINTHIANS 1:10

A man will leave his father and mother and be united to his wife, and they will become one flesh.

GENESIS 2:24

How good and pleasant it is
    when brothers live together in unity!

PSALM 133:1

Unity

He who unites himself with the Lord is one with him in spirit.

1 CORINTHIANS 6:17

It was God who gave some to be apostles, some to be prophets, some to be evangelists, and some to be pastors and teachers, to prepare God's people for works of service, so that the body of Christ may be built up until we all reach unity in the faith and in the knowledge of the Son of God and become mature, attaining to the whole measure of the fullness of Christ.

EPHESIANS 4:11–13

If you have any encouragement from being united with Christ, if any comfort from his love, if any fellowship with the Spirit, if any tenderness and compassion, then make my joy complete by being like-minded, having the same love, being one in spirit and purpose.

PHILIPPIANS 2:1–2

Unity

GENESIS 2:24

In the beginning, God created a lifelong relationship between a man and a woman, and he called it "marriage." Intended as the closest and most satisfying of all human relationships, the marriage bond remains strong when we follow the three principles found in this passage: leaving, cleaving and becoming one.

Leaving our families was the easy part for us. All I wanted was to be with Dave! Even pulling off a wedding between Christmas and New Year's was simple. But after the wedding, we were unprepared for the struggles we encountered. Family wasn't all we needed to leave, and it wasn't a one-time event. Over the years for us, leaving has involved realigning our priorities from what "I want for me" to what "we want for us"; this has included staying in the relationship through the hard times, being faithful to each other and putting our relationship before other things like our jobs, hobbies and other interests.

The second challenge we faced in our marriage was to learn how to cleave to each other and to become soul mates. It's not easy to be vulnerable to another person—to open up and share intimate thoughts and feelings, and to be willing to give and receive emotional support—but it's the only way to become best friends.

Becoming one involves being skilled lovers. God created the sexual relationship, and it is with God's approval that, in the framework of marriage, we act on our passions for each other. In marriage we experience this unique oneness. When we think about what we might still need to leave behind and consider steps to build a closer friendship, we can add passion to our love life. In the beginning God created marriage. And it can be very good!

DAVE AND CLAUDIA ARP

GOD'S WORDS OF LIFE ON
Wisdom

The fear of the LORD is the beginning of wisdom;
    all who follow his precepts have good under-
    standing.

PSALM 111:10

The wisdom that comes from heaven is first of all
pure; then peace-loving, considerate, submissive, full
of mercy and good fruit, impartial and sincere.

JAMES 3:17

I thought, "Age should speak;
    advanced years should teach wisdom."
But it is the spirit in a man,
    the breath of the Almighty, that gives him
    understanding.

JOB 32:7–8

Wisdom is sweet to your soul;
    if you find it, there is a future hope for you,
and your hope will not be cut off.

PROVERBS 24:14

Wisdom

To God belong wisdom and power;
　　counsel and understanding are his.

JOB 12:13

You desire truth in the inner parts, O LORD;
　　you teach me wisdom in the inmost place.

PSALM 51:6

To the man who pleases him, God gives wisdom,
knowledge and happiness.

ECCLESIASTES 2:26

When pride comes, then comes disgrace,
　　but with humility comes wisdom.

PROVERBS 11:2

Let us learn together what is good.

JOB 34:4

Teach me your way, O LORD,
　　and I will walk in your truth;
give me an undivided heart.

PSALM 86:11

GOD'S WORDS OF LIFE ON
Wisdom

I pray ... that the eyes of your heart may be enlightened in order that you may know the hope to which he has called you, the riches of his glorious inheritance in the saints, and his incomparably great power for us who believe.

EPHESIANS 1:18–19

Do not forsake wisdom, and she will protect you;
    love her, and she will watch over you.

PROVERBS 4:6

The LORD was pleased that Solomon had asked for wisdom. So God said to him, "Since you have asked for this and not for long life or wealth for yourself, nor have asked for the death of your enemies but for discernment in administering justice, I will do what you have asked. I will give you a wise and discerning heart, so that there will never have been anyone like you, nor will there ever be. Moreover, I will give you what you have not asked for—both riches and honor—so that in your lifetime you will have no equal among kings. And if you walk in my ways and obey my statutes and commands as David your father did, I will give you a long life."

1 KINGS 3:10–14

Wisdom

How much better to get wisdom than gold,
    to choose understanding rather than silver!

PROVERBS 16:16

If any of you lacks wisdom, he should ask God, who gives generously to all without finding fault, and it will be given to him.

JAMES 1:5

God chose the foolish things of the world to shame the wise; God chose the weak things of the world to shame the strong. He chose the lowly things of this world and the despised things—and the things that are not—to nullify the things that are, so that no one may boast before him. It is because of him that you are in Christ Jesus, who has become for us wisdom from God—that is, our righteousness, holiness and redemption.

1 CORINTHIANS 1:27–30

Jesus said to his disciples, "I will give you words and wisdom that none of your adversaries will be able to resist or contradict."

LUKE 21:15

Wisdom

Jesus said, "Everyone who hears these words of mine and puts them into practice is like a wise man who built his house on the rock. The rain came down, the streams rose, and the winds blew and beat against that house; yet it did not fall, because it had its foundation on the rock."

MATTHEW 7:24–25

Those who are wise will shine like the brightness of the heavens, and those who lead many to righteousness, like the stars for ever and ever.

DANIEL 12:3

Wisdom is better than strength.

ECCLESIASTES 9:16

Wisdom

---

1 KINGS 3

Marriage comes with a built-in reality check. We ask questions of our spouse like, "Do you think I sounded too flippant when John asked me about my job?" or "Do you think I don't smile enough?" And sometimes our partner says things like, "Honey, you tend to jump to conclusions at times." or "Do you realize how much you worry about that?" Questions and comments like these emerge naturally in a healthy marriage, and they can be a source for personal growth and wisdom.

Maybe that's what Solomon meant by a discerning heart. Instead of asking God for riches and honor, he asked for wisdom. That's not a bad idea for couples. When was the last time you asked God for wisdom in your marriage? If you are like most couples, it may have been a while. Read how the Lord responded to Solomon's request (see verses 10–14). God would like to do the same for you.

LES AND LESLIE PARROTT

Working Together

Two are better than one,
>   because they have a good return for their
>   work:
If one falls down,
>   his friend can help him up.
But pity the man who falls
>   and has no one to help him up! ...
Though one may be overpowered,
>   two can defend themselves.
A cord of three strands is not quickly broken.

ECCLESIASTES 4:9–10, 12

Do not work for food that spoils, but for food that
endures to eternal life, which the Son of Man will
give you.

JOHN 6:27

God who began a good work in you will carry it on
to completion until the day of Christ Jesus.

PHILIPPIANS 1:6

God is not unjust; he will not forget your work and
the love you have shown him as you have helped his
people and continue to help them.

HEBREWS 6:10

Working Together

Do your best to present yourself to God as one approved, a workman who does not need to be ashamed and who correctly handles the word of truth.

2 TIMOTHY 2:15

Now we ask you . . . to respect those who work hard among you, who are over you in the Lord and who admonish you. Hold them in the highest regard in love because of their work. Live in peace with each other.

1 THESSALONIANS 5:12–13

We continually remember before our God and Father your work produced by faith, your labor prompted by love, and your endurance inspired by hope in our Lord Jesus Christ.

1 THESSALONIANS 1:3

Whatever you do, work at it with all your heart, as working for the Lord, not for men, since you know that you will receive an inheritance from the Lord as a reward. It is the Lord Christ you are serving.

COLOSSIANS 3:23–24

Working Together

Continue to work out your salvation with fear and trembling, for it is God who works in you to will and to act according to his good purpose.

PHILIPPIANS 2:12–13

It was God who gave some to be apostles, some to be prophets, some to be evangelists, and some to be pastors and teachers, to prepare God's people for works of service, so that the body of Christ may be built up until we all reach unity in the faith and in the knowledge of the Son of God and become mature, attaining to the whole measure of the fullness of Christ. ... From him the whole body, joined and held together by every supporting ligament, grows and builds itself up in love, as each part does its work.

EPHESIANS 4:11–13, 16

Working Together

PSALM 20:4

Wouldn't it be great if all of our plans succeeded and we always got our heart's desire? While trusting God doesn't guarantee success, wise couples plan and set goals for their marriage. No matter how long you have been married, taking an annual check-up and setting goals can be beneficial.

First look at your marriage as it is now. In your relationship, which of your heart desires have you already experienced? Second, consider what areas in your relationship need some work. Think about what you can do to strengthen these and choose one to start with. End your check-up by looking toward the future. What are our hopes and dreams—what are you looking forward to?

Marriage check-ups don't have to be complicated. You can have one almost anywhere. Once we did a check-up on a paper placemat over potato skins and two glasses of iced tea. We talked about some of the positive aspects of our marriage such as our good communication, flexibility, sense of adventure, ability to laugh together and our love life. Next we discussed areas we need to work on and picked one—getting more exercise—to start with. Later, we talked about things we are looking forward to this next year. We proclaimed that this year we are going to reorganize—starting with a bedroom make over.

Now it's your turn. Ask for God's blessing on your goals and be open to how he may adapt them to fit your true needs.

DAVE AND CLAUDIA ARP

Worry

But blessed is the man who trusts in the LORD,
    whose confidence is in him.
He will be like a tree planted by the water
    that sends out its roots by the stream.
It does not fear when heat comes;
    its leaves are always green.
It has no worries in a year of drought
    and never fails to bear fruit.

JEREMIAH 17:7–8

Jesus said, "Do not worry about your life, what you
will eat or drink; or about your body, what you will
wear. Is not life more important than food, and the
body more important than clothes? Look at the
birds of the air; they do not sow or reap or store
away in barns, and yet your heavenly Father feeds
them. Are you not much more valuable than they?
Who of you by worrying can add a single hour to
his life?"

MATTHEW 6:25–27

When anxiety was great within me,
    your consolation brought joy to my soul,
    O LORD.

PSALM 94:19

Worry

An anxious heart weighs a man down,
    but a kind word cheers him up.

PROVERBS 12:25

Do not be anxious about anything, but in everything, by prayer and petition, with thanksgiving,
present your requests to God. And the peace of God,
which transcends all understanding, will guard your
hearts and your minds in Christ Jesus.

PHILIPPIANS 4:6–7

Cast all your anxiety on God because he cares for
you.

1 PETER 5:7

I call on the LORD in my distress,
    and he answers me.

PSALM 120:1

In all their distress [the Messiah] too was distressed,
    and the angel of his presence saved them.
In his love and mercy he redeemed them;
    he lifted them up and carried them
    all the days of old.

ISAIAH 63:9

Worry

In my distress I called to the LORD;
> I called out to my God.
From his temple he heard my voice;
> my cry came to his ears.
The earth trembled and quaked,
> the foundations of the heavens shook;
> they trembled because he was angry. . . .
He parted the heavens and came down;
> dark clouds were under his feet.
He mounted the cherubim and flew;
> he soared on the wings of the wind. . . .
Out of the brightness of his presence
> bolts of lightning blazed forth.
The LORD thundered from heaven;
> the voice of the Most High resounded.
He shot arrows and scattered the enemies,
> bolts of lightning and routed them. . . .
He reached down from on high and took hold of me;
> he drew me out of deep waters.
He rescued me from my powerful enemy,
> from my foes, who were too strong for me.
They confronted me in the day of my disaster,
> but the LORD was my support.
He brought me out into a spacious place;
> he rescued me because he delighted in me.

2 SAMUEL 22:7–8, 10–11, 13–15, 17–20

Worry

The LORD your God is with you,
    he is mighty to save.
He will take great delight in you,
    he will quiet you with his love,
    he will rejoice over you with singing.

ZEPHANIAH 3:17

Let the beloved of the LORD rest secure in him,
    for he shields him all day long,
    and the one the LORD loves rests between
    his shoulders.

DEUTERONOMY 33:12

I have set the LORD always before me.
    Because he is at my right hand,
    I will not be shaken.
Therefore my heart is glad and my tongue rejoices;
    my body also will rest secure.

PSALM 16:8–9

He who fears the LORD has a secure fortress,
    and for his children it will be a refuge.

PROVERBS 14:26

Worry

Jesus said, "And why do you worry about clothes?
See how the lilies of the field grow. They do not
labor or spin. Yet I tell you that not even Solomon in
all his splendor was dressed like one of these. If that
is how God clothes the grass of the field, which is
here today and tomorrow is thrown into the fire,
will he not much more clothe you? . . . So do not
worry, saying, 'What shall we eat?' or 'What shall we
drink?' or 'What shall we wear?' For . . . your heavenly Father knows that you need them. But seek first
his kingdom and his righteousness, and all these
things will be given to you as well."

MATTHEW 6:28–33

Worry

JOHN 6:16–21

Financial hardship was one of the best things to happen to our marriage. During our newlywed years, finances were extremely tight. Initially, the thought of not being able to pay our bills scared [us] to death. But the potential time of fear actually became a strong gluing element in our marriage. ...

In their night at sea, the disciples had to learn three steps in dealing with their fear. They learned to pull together, to do their best and to look for Jesus. In our nights of fear we must do the same. A couple must "glue" together rather than allow the fear to blow them apart. Then as they pray and talk over their options, they must then do their best to deal with the difficulty. Most of all, each couple needs to know that Jesus will come to them. He may not come in the way you expect him or have requested him to come; but he will come to your aid. When a couple accepts that as a fact, then they can avoid being debilitated by the emotion of fear. There is nothing to fear when we know that Jesus will rescue us.

BOB AND ROSEMARY BARNES

Worship

You turned my wailing into dancing;
>   you removed my sackcloth
and clothed me with joy,
>   that my heart may sing to you
and not be silent.
>   O LORD my God, I will give you thanks forever.

PSALM 30:11–12

I run in the path of your commands, O LORD,
>   for you have set my heart free.

PSALM 119:32

Praise the LORD.
I will extol the LORD with all my heart
>   in the council of the upright and in the assembly.
Great are the works of the LORD;
>   they are pondered by all who delight in them.

PSALM 111:1–2

Therefore, since we are receiving a kingdom that
cannot be shaken, let us be thankful, and so worship
God acceptably with reverence and awe.

HEBREWS 12:28

Worship

As the deer pants for streams of water,
    so my soul pants for you, O God.
My soul thirsts for God, for the living God.
    When can I go and meet with God?

PSALM 42:1–2

Your righteousness reaches to the skies, O God,
    you who have done great things.
Who, O God, is like you? . . .
    you will restore my life again;
from the depths of the earth you will again bring
    me up.
You will increase my honor
    and comfort me once again.
I will praise you with the harp
    for your faithfulness, O my God;
I will sing praise to you with the lyre,
    O Holy One of Israel.
My lips will shout for joy
    when I sing praise to you—
    I, whom you have redeemed.
My tongue will tell of your righteous acts
    all day long.

PSALM 71:19–24

Worship

I urge you, ... in view of God's mercy, to offer your bodies as living sacrifices, holy and pleasing to God—this is your spiritual act of worship. Do not conform any longer to the pattern of this world, but be transformed by the renewing of your mind.

ROMANS 12:1–2

Say to God, "How awesome are your deeds!
    So great is your power ...
All the earth bows down to you;
    they sing praise to you,
    they sing praise to your name."
Come and see what God has done,
    how awesome his works in man's behalf!
He turned the sea into dry land,
    they passed through the waters on foot—
    come, let us rejoice in him. ...
Praise our God, O peoples,
    let the sound of his praise be heard.

PSALM 66:3–6, 8

Worship

Deep calls to deep
    in the roar of your waterfalls;
all your waves and breakers
    have swept over me.
By day the LORD directs his love,
    at night his song is with me—
    a prayer to the God of my life.

PSALM 42:7–8

This I call to mind
    and therefore I have hope:
Because of the LORD's great love we are not con-
    sumed,
    for his compassions never fail.
They are new every morning;
    great is your faithfulness.
I say to myself, "The LORD is my portion;
    therefore I will wait for him."
The LORD is good to those whose hope is in him,
    to the one who seeks him;
it is good to wait quietly
    for the salvation of the LORD.

LAMENTATIONS 3:21–26

Worship

All the angels were standing around the throne and around the elders and the four living creatures. They fell down on their faces before the throne and worshiped God, saying:

"Amen!
Praise and glory
and wisdom and thanks and honor
and power and strength
be to our God for ever and ever.
Amen!"

REVELATION 7:11–12

Worship

Perhaps nothing reflects who we are as much as the way in which we express our most intimate thoughts about God. He deserves our most honest and sincere worship. Psalms is a collection of prayers and songs written by a variety of authors who voice a wide range of human emotion—joy, excitement, compassion, love, anger, grief, and even depression.

The Psalms help us discover what it means to be "real" with God, for we often hear our own emotions reflected in these timeless songs. Through the Psalms we discover what it means to "worship [him] in spirit and truth" (John 4:24). Select a psalm that expresses your thoughts about God. Now read that psalm aloud to your spouse as a way to be "real" with God together.

MARRIAGE DEVOTIONAL BIBLE

Marriage checkup

God desires your marriage to be a healthy one. He is committed to you and to the success of your marriage. To give your marriage a health check, answer the following questions together:

1. What are three things that are positive about our marriage?

2. What are two things about our marriage that are OK, but could be better?

3. What is one thing we each could do on our own to improve our marriage?

Marriage prayer

Lord, we lift up this prayer to you for our marriage ...

_____

_____

_____

_____

_____

_____

_____

_____

_____

_____

_____

_____

_____

_____

_____

_____

_____

About the authors

Dave and Claudia Arp are the founders and directors of Marriage Alive International, a marriage and family enrichment ministry. They've authored several books, including *The Second Half of Marriage* and *10 Great Dates*.

Bob and Rosemary Barnes run a residential treatment center for juvenile delinquent boys and girls. They also have a ministry for single moms. Together they have authored *Great Sexpectations, We Need to Talk,* and *Rock-Solid Marriage*.

Les and Leslie Parrott are co-directors of the Center for Relationship Development at Seattle Pacific University. It's a ground-breaking program dedicated to teaching the basics of good relationships. They have authored *Becoming Soul Mates, Saving Your Marriage Before It Starts,* and *Questions Couples Ask*.